FABIAN SOCIALISM

FABIAN SOCIALISM

by

G. D. H. COLE

Routledge
Taylor & Francis Group
LONDON AND NEW YORK

First published 1971 by
FRANK CASS AND COMPANY LIMITED

Published 2014 by Routledge
2 Park Square, Milton Park, Abingdon, Oxfordshire OX14 4RN
711 Third Avenue, New York, NY 10017

First issued in paperback 2014

Routledge is an imprint of the Taylor & Francis Group, an informa business

First published	April 1943
Second impression	May 1943
Third impression	1971

Transferred to Digital Printing 2006

ISBN 978-0-714-61553-0 (hbk)
ISBN 978-1-138-87464-0 (pbk)

Publisher's Note
The publisher has gone to great lengths to ensure the quality of this reprint but points out that some imperfections in the original may be apparent

PREFACE

I BEGAN writing this book in August, 1941, when I was at the Fabian Society's Summer School at Dartington Hall. I was moved to write it by the insistent demand which was there made for a new Socialist crusade, based on a new interpretation of Socialism in the light of the conditions created by the war. We were all then in a mood of excitement and emotional exaltation, stimulated by the recent attack of the Nazis on the Soviet Union, and by the news that was coming through daily of the magnificent, but at that time seemingly desperate, resistance offered by the Red Army to the onslaughts on Leningrad and Moscow. We felt that, though we could do little directly at that stage to help the Russians in their struggle, it was at any rate our affair, as Socialists, to hold out to them the hand of comradeship, and to do all we could to create in this country a Socialist movement which would be capable of playing a proper part in winning both the war and the peace.

Out of that gathering much more than this book was born. Since the autumn of 1941, the Fabian Society, on the strength of its revived work for Socialism, has been gaining members and influence at an unprecedented rate; and local Fabian Societies have been springing into existence all over the country as fast as we have been able to organise them. The Society has issued, in a booklet entitled *A Word on the Future to British Socialists*, its own re-interpretation of Socialist ideas and doctrine in the light of present-day conditions; and I have myself told something of its current activities in a second booklet, *The Fabian Society, Past and Present*.

A much longer time than I anticipated has gone by before it has been possible to get the present volume into the hands of the public. This has given me the opportunity of revising it in a number of respects; but one outstanding event, the publication of the Beveridge Report on the Social Services, occurred after the manuscript had finally left my hands. Actually, the chapter of my book dealing with Social Security

('A Chance for Everybody') was finished in 1941, and has not been touched since. I mention this point only because its close similarity at many points to the Beveridge proposals might lead to a suspicion of unacknowledged plagiarism if I did not. My chapter was also written before, and quite independently of, the important evidence submitted by the Fabian Society's Social Security Committee to the Beveridge Committee—evidence since published under the title of *Social Security*, and also bearing a remarkably close resemblance in many of its features to what Sir William Beveridge has proposed.

I ought to add that my book, despite its title, is not to be regarded as in any sense an official Fabian publication. I happen to be Chairman of the Fabian Executive; but the views expressed are mine, and they have no responsibility for them. My views are not to be regarded as 'orthodox' Fabianism; for the Fabian Society, I am glad to say, has no orthodoxy. It is a free-thinking body of 'liberal' Socialists, in the sense in which I have used the word 'liberal' in this book; and I hope most Fabians will agree with most of what I have said. But this is only a hope, and not an assertion. May I add to it the further hope that those who agree broadly with the spirit of what I have written will join the Fabian Society and, by working through it for *sensible* Socialism, help to make of it the engine of mental revolution of which the British people stands in urgent need.

G. D. H. COLE.

HENDON,
December, 1942.

CONTENTS

I

PERSONS AND POLITICS

Some day, quite soon, when this war is over and the Nazis have been beaten and the terror lifted from the peoples, you and I, if we are still alive, will have to rebuild England. I say 'England', because I am an Englishman and feel that in England is my home and my land of heart's desire. But, though I say 'England', I mean, and have to mean, much more; for how can we hope to build a happy England in an unhappy and distracted world? If I were a Scot, or a Welshman, or an Ulsterman, I expect I should think first of all of Scotland, or of Wales, or of Northern Ireland (or perhaps of Ireland as a whole). If I were a Frenchman or a German or a Russian, I should think first of my own country—of the sort of life I want to live in it, and the lives I want my fellow-countrymen to be able to lead. But, from whatever point my thoughts began, and to whatever point they came continually back, I should have to think about other countries as well as my own. For there is nothing more positive than that, of whatever country I feel myself a citizen, the fate of my country is bound up with what happens to the world at large.

I wish I did not have to think in this enlarged way; for it makes thinking very difficult. It would be hard enough to plan out a decent future for England, and to find ways of acting with my fellow-Englishmen so as to make our dreams come true, without troubling our heads about the affairs of other countries. It is none too easy a matter to make up one's mind how England ought to be governed, or how we should set about the task of rebuilding England after the devastations of war. But enough has occurred in our own day, and is happening even now, to show us clearly that we cannot succeed if we plan for ourselves alone. We all but brought sheer destruction upon our country by not planning with others how to prevent Hitler's aggression—that is, by our failure to form a common front of peace-loving countries strong enough to make Hitler afraid of attacking them. That failure has cost us the misery into which we are plunged to-day; and it should be plain to all of us that there can be no secure escape from such misery unless, in beating Hitler, we also make and carry out effective plans for enabling all Europe to live in peace and friendship in the coming times.

We have, then, to attend to the affairs of Europe, and of the whole world, as well as to those which are more particularly our own. But, for most of us, though this is true, the main responsibility is connected with the affairs of our own country. For we cannot, except by helping our utmost to defeat the Nazis, *do* much about the rest of the world, whereas we can do a great deal to affect what happens here in England. We shall do what we are called upon to do here all the better if we do it with insight into what our actions mean for the citizens of other countries, and if we act with the feeling that we are their comrades in a common task. But our chance of acting is bound to be mainly—the actual fighting apart—a chance of acting here, in our own country; and it is mainly through what we do in our own country that we can hope to affect the world.

But can we do anything? Very many men and women are inclined to say that, in times such as these, there is really nothing they can do. Of course I do not mean literally nothing; for at present most of them are working very hard. They are in the armed forces, or the home defence services, or the munition factories or mines, or the merchant marine, or in some other of the countless branches of activity that make up the war effort. Or perhaps they are carrying on with their ordinary peace-time jobs, in the knowledge that these are no less indispensable, and are working a good deal harder than usual because so many of those who used to work with them have been taken away for services more directly connected with the war.

Most of us, in one way or another, are working exceptionally hard in these days; and when we do get a few hours off we are apt to feel that we thoroughly deserve a rest. But if those who read this book feel at all like me—and I fully believe many of them do—they do not find it so easy after all to take a rest when the chance comes. For rest, in order to be really restful, demands some peace of mind. Whereas, when I try to rest nowadays, there come into my mind all sorts of worries that nag at me, and forbid me to achieve a real peace of spirit. No doubt it is possible to get rid, for the moment, of these sensations—to drive them out of the active consciousness for the time being by absorbing oneself in something else; for example, by dancing, or by listening to fine music, or by doing whatever most takes you out of yourself according to the way you are made. But that is not a satisfying answer to the problem; for no sooner is the excitement over than the worries begin again to nag at you, perhaps the more insistently because you have succeeded, for a little while, in putting them out of your mind.

Doubtless this experience presses upon some of us much more hardly than upon others, at any rate in the sense that some of us are much more aware of it. But I believe it does press, to an important extent, on nearly all of us, or at least upon all normally decent and sensitive people. It can affect us without our being clearly conscious of it, setting up an uneasiness which makes us fidgety, or spoils our tempers, or gives us a craving for excitement, or causes us to dream and to sleep less soundly than we used to do. Of this I am sure, that this kind of experience affects us most keenly when we feel lonely and, in our loneliness, afraid.

Our worries and uneasiness can, of course, take many different shapes. Most of us are not worrying, for most of the time, about anything that is ordinarily called 'Politics'; for 'Politics' play only a tiny part in the thoughts of the vast majority of men and women. Most of us are worrying chiefly about what is to happen to our own lives and to the lives of those who are dear to us—husbands or wives, children, parents and friends. We are wondering and worrying, not only what is happening to those whom we love now, or will happen to them before the war is over, but also what sort of life is in store for them when the fighting, and the munition-making, and the *blitz*, and the evacuation are at an end, and we all come to settling down again to a more normal way of living. We are wondering and worrying about our jobs. Will they be there for us to go back to, if we want them? Will the little shop that has been forced to close down ever reopen? Will the factory where we used to work ever want our services again? Will our house that has been destroyed be rebuilt for us just as it was, or better, or worse? Where are we likely to live after the war, and what are we likely to do? Shall we be better or worse off, either absolutely or in comparison with our neighbours? And even—What shall we *want* to do when the fighting is over? Will post-war England be much the same sort of place to live in as the England of the past? Or will it be different; and, if so, how?

Ordinarily, the vast majority of men and women pass their lives in a routine that changes little from week to week. In the course of their lives they make a few decisions which are of vital importance to their happiness—what trade to enter, whom to marry, whether to put up with what comes to them or take risks in the hope of improving their lot. But such decisions are relatively few, and some even of them are taken, for good or ill, almost without thought. When they have been taken, they usually settle the course of our lives for long periods, leaving us with a fixed environment to which we fit ourselves in as best we can. Most of us, for most of the time, take this environment for granted; and the older we get the smaller usually our power of varying it becomes.

At present, however, that condition no longer holds good. We may be living as much under a daily routine as ever, or even more. But the routine is not one which we expect to last. We are going on from it to something different, which may be the old routine we have left, or something akin to it, but may also be very widely apart from any way of living we have ever known. We cannot see, as we mostly think we can in ordinary times, what the future—*our* future—is going to be like. That gives us a feeling of being lost, in a world which has ceased to have fixed landmarks for us, or even signposts by which we can find our way.

I have suggested that this sense of being lost affects us most when we feel most alone. Now, *feeling* alone is a very different thing from *being* alone, in a physical sense. A person can feel quite horribly alone, like a child that has strayed from its parents, in the midst of a huge crowd. The loneliness that matters is not physical isolation in itself, but the absence of fellowship. In our ordinary lives we have families and friends with whom we consort, and with whom we are partners in certain settled and regular enterprises, such as keeping a home, or cultivating common tastes and interests, or furthering a common cause. But now many of us have been torn away from these familiar environments and contacts, or, even if we remain in them, feel their foundations rocking under our feet. Even if we can in all sincerity write home to say that we are feeling fine, and having a good time, on the whole, there is often at the back of our professions a gnawing doubt. What is it all leading to, after all? What is to happen to us when the Government and the Generals have done with treating us as pawns in the military game? What is it all *for*; and what are we *for*? And why should this idiotic upset have been allowed to happen?

Thus, our thoughts about our own future, about our private lives and the lives of our families and friends, lead us on to wider questions, which are 'Politics,' whether we call them by that name or not. But at this point loneliness is most apt to afflict us, and to prevent us from seeing or thinking straight. Men in camp or barracks will swap tales about home, show one another their kiddies' pictures, and, in moments of confidence, pour out some of their personal perplexities to those whom they find most congenial among their fellow-exiles from home. The same thing will happen in air-raid shelters, or in factories on night-shift, when the discipline is relaxed, or, quite casually, when strangers meet on a journey and get to talking frankly with no expectation of ever meeting again. But most of this talking is about personal and private affairs, and very little, as far as I can judge, about politics. Or, rather, what political talk there is comes out of the newspapers, and is mere surface froth, and not a real exchange of opinion. Men pick up newspaper notions of what is being mismanaged here or there, of this or that Minister's incompetence, of this or that change that needs to be made; and they pass such notions on, as small talk, without attaching any real importance to them, or regarding themselves personally as having any sort of responsibility in relation to them. Of course, this does not apply to everybody. There are politically minded individuals everywhere—in camp or barracks, on board ship, in the factories, and in the pubs. But they are a small minority; the great majority of men talk much more seriously, and think very much more seriously, about private than about public affairs.

Up to a point, women talk about politics more seriously than men. For war-time politics—food rationing, clothes rationing, and most of the forms of 'State control'—put up more urgent practical problems to the housewives than to any other section of the people. To some extent, the ordinary rôles are reversed: women in war-time become more political, and men less. But the women too, for the most part, only exchange grumbles and expedients: most of them do not regard these things as matters about which they are called upon to act in any political way.

Man has been defined as by nature a 'political animal'; and so in a sense he is. It is a necessity for him to live in communities; and it is very rare to find a man who can be happy when he is long alone. Solitary confinement is a most terrible punishment: men are gregarious by nature, and for most of them it is a good deal easier to speak to others than to themselves. Thinking in solitude is a highly advanced art; and for most men such thinking can go but a very little way. But 'gregariousness', which is natural to men, is a very different thing from 'politicalness', in any sense one would ordinarily attach to being 'political'. Being 'political' seems to imply a disposition to take in hand positively the management of the common affairs of a group; and in this sense the vast majority of Englishmen are certainly not political, or are so only to a very tiny extent.

The consequence is that when ordinary men and women find themselves led on of necessity from thinking about their own and their families' future to thinking about the social environment in which their lives are to be led, they are apt to feel very helpless. In a relatively stable world they were able to take this environment for granted; and most of them did. But they cannot take it for granted now, because the world they knew and lived in has, for very many of them, been torn up by the roots. They are lost and bewildered; and as they have not been in the habit of taking politics seriously, and do not know what to think about them now, they find the greatest difficulty in even beginning to exchange real ideas upon such matters with those they meet. They continue to exchange trivialities of second-hand newspaper jargon when they approach such themes. They can talk fairly easily about their personal affairs, and mean what they say, because in relation to them they know, broadly speaking, what they want and where they stand. In political matters they do not know; and the superficial talk which they exchange mostly means nothing real to them or to their hearers.

We English are, indeed, in these days an extraordinarily unpolitical people. We were not always so. There was a time when nearly every public-house in a working-class district was a centre of keen political dispute, when farmers' 'ordinaries' nearly came to blows about the rights and wrongs of Whig and Tory policies, and when the voteless people was much more alive to political issues than the great majority of voters are to-day. There was a time when religion was a great political force, and ordinary men held their political opinions with a zeal which seemed to them to come from God. We English have great traditions of our past battles for political liberty, and pride ourselves on our achievements as pioneers in the democratic cause. Our Parliament is the 'Mother of Parliaments'; and we have still a way of regarding most foreigners as vastly our inferiors in the arts of government and political freedom. But of late the zeal has gone out of us; and, taking these things very much for granted, most of us have ceased bothering our heads about them. We have come to thinking of politics, when we think at all, as the other fellow's business, not our own. We still listen in to politicians talking about freedom and democracy; but it no longer occurs to most of us that the defence of these things is our personal and important concern. We have gone slack about politics—or had, until the war; and I do not see much sign that we have become less slack about them even now.

The explanation of this slackness is, I think, to be found partly in the very success with which, in such countries as ours, man has pursued his conquest of the powers of nature. The ability to produce wealth has increased so fast that we have, as a nation, got past the sheer scramble for the means of living which marked the earlier phases of the struggle to live; and, despite the class system, an appreciable part of the new wealth has filtered down to the main body of the people. Even in my own time there has been a quite astonishing change for the better in the material condition of the poor. There are far fewer ragged children or adults, far fewer persons going about filthy or with an evident look of under-nourishment or physical defect, far fewer 'down and outs' or hopeless 'drunks' who have lost all self-respect, far fewer tattered, draggled, anti-social objects who, if they rouse our pity, are bound at the same time to provoke the distaste of ordinary people. The lump of human misery has grown smaller; and, even more, it has become less obtrusive. It is now, except in relatively few places, nearly invisible except to those who deliberately seek it out. This change is due in part to a real diminution in the sum of wretchedness—an outcome of better wages and working conditions, better social services, and better knowledge and education. It is also partly due to the greater expertness of the modern world in tucking misery away where it need not be seen—in institutions for the sick, the disabled, the aged, and the feeble-minded, and in unvisited slum quarters of our overgrown cities. But the fact remains that the sum of sheer physical wretchedness has decreased, and that with its decrease the passion to give the bottom dog a better chance has lost much of its insistence in the minds of those who are better off: so that the very improvements that have been made weaken the social will to advance further.

This, however, is by no means the whole story. It does largely account for the weakening of the impulse to help the wretched; for that impulse is much more easily aroused by the actual sight of misery walking the streets than by any knowledge, got from books or speeches, of its existence. To see unfortunate children, clothed in rags and with the signs of starvation in every inch of them, was much more moving than merely to read about them, especially when it was an incontrovertible fact that their numbers had decreased. The impulses of sheer humanity did grow weaker as they were less keenly stimulated by eye and nose; and men did grow more callous to sufferings which they did not have to see. But the political outlook was never wholly humanitarian: it was an affair of rights as well as of sympathies.

Here, too, the passion waned, partly, as more and more people won the vote for which they had clamoured, and found it not so great a matter after all. The lack of a vote is a much greater stigma than the possession of it is a privilege; and, though men might rise to defend their rights if anyone threatened to take their votes away, this does not cause them to set great store by the suffrage as long as their claim to it is not challenged. Besides this cause of the waning of political passion, there has been another—the apparently settled character of the social system. It may seem strange to say this in face of the immense amount of social legislation that has been crammed into the last thirty or so years. But it is true. Up to the outbreak of war in 1914, even despite the labour unrest and the violent suffragist activities of the years just before the war, the whole social system of Great Britain did appear stable and settled to such a degree that no major change in it seemed to most people likely within the lifetime of any person then living. The war of 1914 to 1918 for a time upset this feeling of stability; but when Germany had been defeated and the British social system was seen to be left intact the feeling reasserted itself, and men came again to take it for granted that the system in which they lived would last their time, and probably their children's too.

This was much less the case in other countries of Europe; but I am speaking here of Great Britain, and, particularly, of England. On the Continent the crisis of 1931 shook every country much more than it shook us; and with the collapse of the German Republic and the advent of Hitler the sense of insecurity became all-pervading. Great Britain, however, came through that crisis, too, almost unshaken, or, rather, unaware of the shock which British institutions had sustained. The ordinary man and woman, though they were made uneasy by the rise of Nazism and could perhaps have been stirred into effective political activity if they had been given the right lead, remained less than half conscious of what was happening, and were not roused to take any action in face of the growing peril. They remained politically apathetic, save a few, and continued to live on the old assumption of a stable environment, even if their confidence in its stability had become less.

Why did the people go on cherishing this belief that they could afford not to bother about politics, because politics could not greatly affect their lives, so long after this view had ceased to be in any sense correct? I have hinted at lack of leadership as part of the explanation, at any rate in the final phase. But why was there no leadership? I am sure the lack was due partly to the increasing extent to which ability was being drained away out of the social classes which were conscious of economic grievance, and was being transferred to administrative or technical positions within the established order. This was a natural consequence both of the changing technique of production, which called for many more skilled underlings in 'staff' positions, and also of the growth of public secondary education, which made it much easier for children of ability to rise to such positions out of the manual working class. These changes left the manual workers the poorer in leadership by taking away their potentially best men; and the individuals who were thus transferred to 'management', so far from feeling a grievance against the system which had promoted them, became in most cases its upholders. Left in the ranks of the manual workers, they would have sought to express themselves by means of political or trade union leadership: given technical or administrative status, they found self-expression in their jobs, and for the most part saw no reason for taking any part in politics. Moreover, to the limited extent to which they did take part, they tended to become conservative, because they were fairly well off as they were, or thought so, and political change looked as if it would mean being bossed by the class out of which they had risen.

This situation suited very neatly the wishes of those who stood for the defence of the established order. The ruling classes in business and politics did not want the people to become ardent Conservatives; for if they had they would have taken to trying to run the Conservative Party. The Conservative leaders wanted the people's votes, but not their political activity between elections; and nothing could have been more convenient for them than a situation which deprived the ordinary workmen of their leaders and diverted the interests of a large proportion of the able men in the country away from politics. As long as this went on, they felt secure in their power to go on governing on 'sound' Conservative lines—as they have actually done.

It is, I imagine, obvious that this ability rests on one assumption—that the economic foundations of the existing order are secure. Where they are not, the outcome of a process of social selection which deprives the people of its natural leaders is not 'sound' Conservatism, but Fascism. For when the non-political men of ability find that economic affairs are going wrong, and that their own status and incomes are seriously threatened, they grow violent in defence of these things and, seeing those who attempt to lead the suffering workers as their most dangerous enemies, demand that such movements as Communism and Socialism and even Trade Unionism be put down with a strong hand. This might happen here; but there has so far been no chance for it to happen because, so far, the stability of the economic foundations of Great Britain has not been shaken in such a way as to cause the superstructure to rock—or, in other words, nothing has occurred to make the main body of technical and administrative workers seriously fear either social revolution or the loss of their jobs on account of economic collapse. Nothing, so far—that is, nothing prior to the outbreak of the war, and nothing since then that is very likely to show above the surface for as long as the war lasts.

There are, however, as we have seen, already many men who have grave fears about what is to happen to them after the war, and some who are suffering present calamity, as well as fear for the future, as an outcome of war conditions. But both the present calamity and the fear at present assail rather the proprietors of small businesses than the salaried technicians and administrators. The small shopkeeper or merchant or workshop master, deprived of his little capital and his business connection, is apt to be a helpless victim: the salaried man, unless he is getting on in years, can with much better hope look round for another job. He will be tolerably all right, as long as jobs are tolerably plentiful: he is not, like the small tradesman or employer, dependent on a single, precarious hold.

These small tradesmen and employers are, politically, very helpless. They are not a class possessing any coherence; and very few of them are politically minded. They have little power to lead or to influence others; and nothing noticeable happens to society even when large numbers of them are ruined. The technical and administrative workers are, potentially, much more formidable. They are on the average much more able, younger and more vigorous, and much more important in the structure of modern society. As long as they remain in general non-political, or politically lukewarm, the level of political passion in the whole community is likely to remain low. On the other hand, if they once become convinced that the foundations of the system by which they live are slipping away under their feet, they will become politically active in self-defence. And they will be formidable in action, whichever side they take—whether they resort to Fascism as a means of bolstering up the threatened economic order or throw in their lot with those who are attempting to build up a different order in its place.

Given a tendency for the people to lose to business pursuits its political leaders, there are other forces which work strongly on the side of a decline in political activity. Among these are the growth in the quantity and variety of cheap amusements—the cinema above all others; the growing distances to be travelled to and from work, which make the home a mere dormitory except at week-ends, and the factory a place to be rushed away from the moment the hour of release strikes; the wireless, which brings news and rumour into the home, instead of sending men to pubs or political meetings; the deliberate emptying of most newspapers of real political content, and the substitution for it of mass-produced triviality; the greater hurry of modern life, which leaves less room for argument and discussion; and the decline of religion, especially in its chapel-going forms. Add to all these sheer numerousness; for the more voters there are the less a single vote seems worth, and it is harder for the politically conscious few to influence great masses than to make their impact upon smaller groups.

Under all these influences the political spirit of the English people has declined. But I am sure it is destined to be aroused again very soon. It was able to decline, without bringing disaster upon us, because the foundations of our society were stable for the time, so that life went on much the same (not quite the same, of course) whether most men were politically active or not. But these foundations are no longer stable: they are utterly insecure. Already, as a result of the war, Great Britain has lost a large part of the overseas investments which have provided much of the income of the richer classes, a large part of its foreign markets, which will not be regained easily where they can be regained at all, and a large part of its shipping. Already the need for man-power for the Services is dislocating the industries which are not fully required for the war effort, and private traders are being ruined in large numbers by shortage of supplies. High taxation can be borne easily enough by those who are making high profits; but it presses very hardly on those whose incomes have been seriously cut down by war conditions. Changes, not yet fully seen or appreciated, are going on in the social structure of the country; and even if the war were to end now, there could be no return to pre-war conditions nearly so complete as tha which took place after 1918. As there is no prospect of an early ending, and every successive month makes the pressure more intense, it seems probable that Great Britain will emerge a very different country, and that the very foundations of the social order will have to be rebuilt. Politics in that event will so closely affect every man's hopes that no one will be able to escape from them. There will be a general revival of political interest and activity. But in what shape?

The opportunity will be great; but so will the danger. The danger will be greatest, and the opportunity least, if they come upon us unprepared. If we have all to act suddenly, without having thought out ahead and in concert what we mean to do, we shall be at the mercy of those small groups who will have thought, and have banded themselves together, for their own ends. Important among these will be the great capitalist trusts and combines, which are already, in the midst of war, planning for the retention of their power, and for its enlargement, in the days to come. Important on the other side will be such small groups as the Communists, who, despite the curious gyrations of their policy, have a determinate political objective, and can reckon on an increase of followers proportionate to the general confusion of affairs. Important may be the Fascists, submerged as they now are; but I fancy the real Fascists of the coming time will not be followers of Sir Oswald Mosley, but will emanate, with big business support, from the ranks of the Conservative Party. Important, in effect, will be all the forces which rely, not on democratically formed opinion coming up from the people, but on plans carefully laid by a few to catch the many—on demagogy, and not on democracy.

This is what will come upon us if we have to face the post-war confusion without being prepared for it in advance. But, for those of us who are democrats, the work of making preparation is no mere matter of drawing up blue prints for the society we want to build, essential as that task is, but much more a matter of preparing ourselves. If we are to seize our opportunity when it comes, and to use it for democratic ends, we must have people, and not merely a plan, prepared. We must spread far and wide among the people both an understanding of the tasks that will have to be done and a will to carry them through to the end. We must not let democracy sleep on the plea that the war must first be won, or we shall infallibly lose the peace.

That is why it is disastrous that the political activities of the Left have been allowed to sink so largely into disuse since the war began. I know there are many excuses. The electoral truce, in both national and local politics, made it seem natural to pack up, for the period of the war, most of the organising and propagandist energy which had been previously devoted so largely to electoral concerns. Why keep an agent, and how raise the funds for him, when there are no contests to be fought? The activity of the Labour Party in particular, as far as it touched the main body of the electorate as distinct from the active groups of political workers, was almost entirely electoral, and disappeared with the outbreak of war. It is no substitute for this to go on holding conferences of the faithful, unless the faithful have means of passing on the inspiration of these gatherings to the main body of the people. Even the conferences lose their inspiration when this is no longer done, or even attempted. The main body of the people knows that there are Socialists in the Government; but it has almost forgotten that the Labour Party exists.

I know, also, that the men and women who were before the war most active in the work of Labour and Socialist propaganda have to a very great extent become absorbed in essential war tasks. They are busy running civil defence, evacuation services, and all sorts of other vital war-time activities. They can plead that they have no time to spare from this work, and that it is not their fault if local Labour and Socialist organisation has gone to pieces in their absence. They can plead this; but can any real Socialists accept this plea, however hardly they are driven?

I, for one, am not prepared to accept it. I am working, as hard as most men, at emergency tasks arising out of the war. It has been difficult to set aside the hours needed for writing this book, or to spare the effort of thought that has gone to its making. But for what am I, or is any of us, intent on winning the war, unless we are to win withal a tolerable peace? I agree that to bring about the defeat of Nazism must be our first objective; for unless we can succeed in that, we fail in everything. But winning the war and winning the peace are not, as I see the matter, really separable objectives. Just as we have to begin here and now replacing the factories which are destroyed by bombing, and rehousing the people who lose their homes, so we have, in order to raise the war effort to its maximum potential, to set about reorganising industries and rearranging our national life in ways which are bound to carry their effects into the post-war period. There is a strong case, in many fields, for a 'War Socialism' which has in it the seeds either of real Socialism or of Fascist totalitarian control—for much the same mechanisms are capable of being applied to utterly discrepant ends. It is fully legitimate for Socialists to press, here and now, for socialistic measures which are calculated to expand war-time production and to improve the spirit of the people by requiring equal sacrifice. Moreover, wherever they do this, it is also fully legitimate for them to do their best to prevent 'War Socialism' from being so practised as to serve as an instrument of Fascism, and to negate the very ideals for which Great Britain purports to be doing battle.

Whether a particular measure of State control leads on to real Socialism or to Fascism is, in the last resort, a matter of the power behind it. If the State's power over the individual is to be increased, what matters is who controls the State. State authority, where the State merely does the bidding of great capitalist groups, is in effect the authority of these groups, and becomes an instrument of monopolist oppression. The same power, wielded by a State which truly reflects the will of the people, is a democratic power; and this second sort of authority is likely to be by far the more effective for winning the war because it can pursue single-mindedly that objective, without being turned aside continually by the pressure of vested interests.

Who shall control the State is, however, mainly, in a country governed by methods that are formally democratic, a question of the alertness and effective bringing to bear of popular opinion. Parliament, despite its inferior and misrepresentative composition, has proved itself a valuable instrument, because it has been able, even under war conditions, to ensure publicity for some grievances, and to compel the Government publicly to defend its measures, wherever they cannot be wholly screened from view on the plea of military necessity. Parliament would be a much more useful instrument if there were at its back a continuously active local organisation, prompting and scrutinising the doings of every department of the Government and of every private agency through which the Government has elected to work.

At present this scrutiny is not effective, mainly because, over large parts of the country, the local political movements have gone out of action. To bring them back into day-to-day activity is worth a great deal of effort, from the standpoint both of improving the quality of war organisation and of preparing for the coming tasks of peace-making and reconstruction. We cannot afford, if we are fighting for democracy, to let those who can work most easily in darkness have matters all their own way.

Nor is this only a question of day-to-day scrutiny of what is being done. It concerns also the very objectives for which the war is being fought. This war, as Socialists see it, is the outcome of capitalism's failure to organise the world aright.

If, throughout the period between the two wars, vested interests had not been allowed to have matters pretty much their own way; if great capitalist combines had not been allowed to organise for scarcity instead of plenty; if the world had not, as a result of their machinations, been plunged into the universal depression of the early 'thirties', it is practically certain that Hitler never need have won power in Germany, and that there need have been no war. This war is the outcome of neuroses following upon bitter suffering: that suffering was the outcome, not of any inevitable deficiency of productive power, but of a disastrous misuse of rapidly expanding resources: that misuse was the outcome of an attempt to persist, under the changed conditions of the twentieth century, with forms of economic organisation which may have served the needs of a past era, but are ridiculously inappropriate to the circumstances of our own time: that persistence was the outcome of a failure of the democracies, even when they had established their formal political rights, to use them as means of subjecting the economic system to the service of their communal ends; and that failure was the outcome of a flagging of the democratic impulse, explicable enough, as we have seen, but none the less disastrous to mankind's hopes of security and decent living.

What, then, is to be done? I, as a Socialist, maintain that we can by no means afford to wait until the war is over before we revive our propaganda for Socialism. For I verily believe that unless we succeed in establishing Socialism as the basis of post-war reconstruction, we are destined to fall under Fascism as the only remaining alternative. The capitalist system, in the forms in which we have hitherto been familiar with it, is dead past all possibility of restoration. It stands condemned by its failure, over the inter-war period, to prevent disastrous depression and unemployment, which have led us into this new war; and it has become, as a result of war, so intertwined with the State as its protector and co-ordinator that hereafter it cannot stand except as the State's partner. But capitalism, walking arm in arm with the State and using the

State's authority to maintain its own, is Fascism; and we have seen that this type of hybrid organisation leads on fatally to war.

If, then, the State as it is becomes, inevitably, the ally of the great capitalist groups in keeping the workers in subjection, we must change the State. But we cannot change it save by creating, while the opportunity remains, a free public opinion capable of exerting pressure upon it, and of turning it into an instrument of the popular will. The State is an instrument: it is at the service of those who gain control of it and use it to serve their ends. As matters stand, the State must serve either the vested interests or the people. But the vested interests are organised, to ensure this service, whereas the people are not. Socialists must organise the people, or perish, as Socialism has perished, for the time being, in both Germany and France. We cannot afford to wait until the war is over, and then organise; for if we do that we shall be defeated, before we have had time to organise, by the vested interests, which are organised already and all the time. They can organise privily: democracy can prepare and organise only by open measures. For their essential instruments are few and easy to handle: the instruments of democracy are nothing other than the courage, intelligence and determination of ordinary men and women who can be imbued with faith in the democratic cause.

This suggests not only that Socialists ought to resume their propaganda at once, and organise openly for the coming struggle, but also how they must do these things. The greatest weapon against the vested interests is that of faith—of devotion among ordinary men and women to an ideal that is worth working for, because it gives life meaning, and lifts the political struggle out of the rut of day-to-day compromises and expedients. The democrats of to-day need to set out to recapture the human enthusiasm of the Socialist pioneers, who wrestled for Socialism because they saw in it, not merely a superior form of economic organisation, but a way of life. The fire of that enthusiasm has sunk very low to-day—so low that men and women who are looking for it (and they are many) are apt to miss Socialism, and yet more the Labour Party, in their search, and take to worshipping any strange god, or any plausible movement, that speaks comfortable words.

Why are we letting so much of this bewildered goodwill run to waste in movements which have in them no realistic content, and no prospect of any achievement going beyond words? Why are most political leaders so supine, so dull, so fearful of heterodoxy, that they repel, instead of welcoming, recruits who are very ready to range themselves on their side? Some of us—old Labour 'stalwarts'—are no doubt very certain that the Labour Party stands for certain solid forces, whereas these others stand for nothing except wishes and vague ideals. Others of us, critical as we are of the Labour Party's failure effectively to lead the people during the present crisis, nevertheless see that there is no alternative to it as a rallying point for the forces of social progress; and, seeing this, remain loyal members of the Party. But it is not enough to be a rallying point: it is also necessary to sound the call to arms, and to welcome those who respond to it with honesty of purpose. Neither of these things is the Labour Party now doing. It is letting Socialist propaganda sleep; and it is even receiving would-be recruits, not with welcome, but with repellent suspicion.

We must change all that. We must go out and preach again, as the pioneers of our movement preached, the simple Socialist gospel. At a time when no man knows what the morrow may bring forth, we must assert afresh the old, unalterable truths—that we are members one of another, and that only by working together in amity and brotherly effort can we hope to achieve security, or to make the best of our common heritage. We must make men see both that peace is indivisible, so that they cannot hope to live in peace themselves until they settle the world's affairs on a basis of durable justice, and that, in their own country, they cannot have security until they ensure that their common estate is administered for their common benefit, and not made the sport of profit-making monopolists, who shun plenty and seek scarcity as the means to dearness and exploitation. We must recreate in our people the spirit that makes men ready to endure all for a cause which transcends their private lives, because it is the cause that gives their lives meaning, and makes them feel that they count in the sum of things, and are not mere specks upon an ocean of unmeaning vastness.

We must recreate the Socialist movement as an ethical faith and not merely as the expression of an economic preference for one form of social organisation over another. For unless we do this, though men may say they agree with us, they will not work for us with the enthusiasm and energy that are able to move mountains. Our generation is looking for a sign—for a call to activity; but we have given to it no sign as yet save a sign to be quiet for fear of embarrassing the Government or annoying the Conservative Party. A truce to such truces! If we are out to beat Hitler by democratic methods, we shall not do so by sitting still.

II

BASIC SOCIALISM

I CALL myself a 'Socialist', and have so called myself ever since I was a boy. I became a Socialist, in those far-off days, because the world which I saw around me seemed, as soon as I began to look at it, to be full of injustice and very badly organised for the promotion of human happiness. I was one of the lucky ones, brought up in a well-to-do household, educated at a good school, and given every chance of thinking for myself by a father who believed in freedom, though he was a Conservative and could never be persuaded that Socialism did not mean 'dividing everything up equally'. I soon realised how exceptional my chances were, and began to wonder why I should be thus favoured. The only answer I could find was that there was no valid reason; and as soon as I had arrived at that answer I began wanting to reorganise society on a basis which would give everybody a decent chance.

That desire soon led me to Socialism, and has remained from that time the basis of my Socialist faith. For I could not, and cannot, see how everyone can be given a decent chance except in a society which is organised on the assumption of equal human rights. I do not mean by this that I suppose all men to be equal; for the phrase has no meaning. Equal in what? Certainly not in cleverness, or bodily attainments, or moral qualities, or capacity for service—or in any combination of these qualities, if one could add up things so different. The doctrine of social equality stands for something quite other than this meaningless assertion that men are equal. It means that all men, and of course all women, ought to be given an equal chance of developing whatever good there is in them, of being reasonably happy in their lives, and of being pleasant to live with—for one man's well-being and happiness are bound up with others', and what makes the individual good and happy helps to make other men good and happy as well.

Of course, the equal chance is not by itself enough. Some

men will miss their chances, and make a mess of their lives. They will be punished for this by their own sense of failure; and there is no need for society to set about punishing them into the bargain, merely because they have failed. In addition to the equal chance for all we need compassion for those who fail to take advantage of it, whether by their own fault or not.

That means to me, and has meant ever since I began to think about politics, that society ought to afford to all its members, irrespective of their virtues or vices, their strength or weakness, a tolerable basic standard of living, high enough to keep them in health and reasonable comfort and to enable them to bring up their children after a fashion that will allow them, in their turn, as far as possible, an equal chance of making the best of their lives. No social measures can give a really equal chance to a child that has the misfortune to be reared in a bad or unhappy home; but society can do its best not to punish the children for the parents' shortcomings. I am not under the illusion that the best forms of social organisation can make everybody healthy and happy; but to recognise the limits of what can be done is no reason for not doing all we can.

These two ideas, of the equal chance for all and of the basic standard of living assured to all, led me to Socialism. I think it was only a little later that I added to them a third—always implicit in my attitude, but not fully realised at first. This third idea was that of democracy, which was inseparably linked in my mind with that of freedom—so that I think of them instinctively as one idea, and not two. By democracy I mean not only that everybody who is not out of his mind ought to have an equal chance of playing his part in public affairs, but also that these affairs ought to be so arranged as to make it easy for as many people as possible to play an active part in them, and further that society ought to encourage the fullest possible open discussion of public affairs, and allow men the greatest practicable liberty to organise for public and private purposes.

Gradually this notion of democratic freedom broadened out

in my mind. It came to mean to me that society ought to be so arranged as to encourage difference, and not merely to tolerate it. It takes many sorts of men and women to make a satisfactory human society; and within certain very wide limits the more men differ the better, not only in tastes and habits but also in opinions. For democratic progress comes of the clash of contending outlooks and opinions. In a growing free society, minorities of to-day become majorities of to-morrow, and it is disastrous to impose uniformity of either thought or conduct. This idea, like all true ideas, has its limits; for there must be a certain underlying community of manners and ways of thinking to hold a society together. But in a healthy society this basic community will establish itself almost without being sought: there is much more danger of overstressing it, so as to crush out individuality, than of insisting on it too little.

Socialism, then, came to stand in my mind for the predominance of these three—or, if you prefer, these four—ideas, the equal chance for all, the basic standard of living assured to all, and democratic freedom. You will observe that there is in all this no single word of what many people suppose to be the fundamental Socialist tenet—that the means of production, distribution and exchange ought to be owned in common by the whole people. There is no word of it, so far, because for me, and I think for nearly all Socialists, common ownership is not an end in itself, but a means of bringing these ends I have spoken of into existence. There is no *absolute* validity about the proposition that the entire community ought to own the means of production. Indeed, I can quite imagine societies for which it would not hold good, and I find it difficult to imagine any society in which *all* the means of production ought to be owned in this way. I can, however, imagine no society which *ought* not to do its best to give to all its members an equal chance, an assured basic standard of living, and as much democratic freedom as possible. These things are *ends*, which all decent men *ought* at all times to desire and attempt to further. The communal ownership of the means of production is a *method* of bringing them about, appropriate in the main to the type of society in which you and I are living, but not in any sense morally imperative in all societies, irrespective of time and place.

Of course, even the ends of which I have spoken can be achieved in any society only in part. They are ends to aim at, and to achieve as far as lies within our power. Taking men as they are, we cannot hope to give everyone an equal chance, or to establish a perfect free democracy. We can hope to assure to all members of our own society, in our own time, a tolerable basic standard of life; but we cannot hope either to make that standard as high as we should wish it to be, or to extend a like standard to all the peoples of the world for a long time to come. We can hope for no more than the speedy banishment from among us of primary poverty in all its forms, and therewith a much nearer approximation to equality of opportunity for all our people, and a great growth among them of the democratic spirit. These, however, are ideals quite high enough to work for; and it will be enough for us if we can say on our death-beds that we have worked for them honestly, and have done our best to give a helping hand to other peoples who have been working for them.

This is a quiet way of stating a conviction which is felt with passion, if it is felt at all. If my reason tells me that this is what I ought to do, my emotions also tell me that this is what I want. I cannot be happy in a world full of unnecessary injustice and misery, unless I am doing what I can to help in putting things to rights. Or, at least, I cannot be happy unless I am doing *something* towards this, even if I do much less than I could. I have a conscience about my fellow-men; and this conscience wars with my private selfishness and laziness, which bid me attend to my own affairs, or let matters slide. I am no saint, to do all I should; but I should be acutely unhappy unless I could say to myself honestly that I am not living to myself alone, or to the narrow circle of those whom I love, but am also trying, though not with all my strength, to lessen the sum of human unhappiness and to promote the cause of democratic freedom.

This, surely, is the common experience. Our opportunities differ; and some of us find better chances of being useful to our fellow-men in a narrow, and others in a wider circle. But, in one way or another, we feel a responsibility for the well-being of our fellows, and are not happy unless we are being of some use. Some people feel this more strongly than others; and some find their sphere of service in personal, and others mainly in public acts. But it is all an expression of the same spirit, resting on a sense of justice and a sympathy with others which are part of the way we are made.

Of course, these sentiments do not make all men Socialists. Socialism implies, among those who profess it by conviction and not by the accident of environment, a keener sense than the ordinary that the ends of social justice and human fraternity need to be promoted by collective action. It implies regarding the State as, potentially, not so much a policeman to keep us in order as a means of promoting the good life. It implies a belief that, even though men cannot be made good or happy by legislation, good laws can greatly improve their chances of being good and happy. It implies a belief that human societies ought to be organised for the benefit of all their members, and not of any limited class or group. It implies therewith the belief that collective action for the common good ought to extend to all things which are both essential to men's happiness and capable of being organised collectively without destroying their essential quality. In particular, it implies a conviction that the economic life of society ought not to be left to the play of private forces, but ought to be organised under some form of public control.

As against this view, it used to be argued that a beneficent Providence had so arranged economic affairs as to cause each man, in pursuing his own private interest, to pursue unwittingly and without conscious purpose the good of all. It used to be said that competition to make profits provided the surest guarantee that the consumers would be well and cheaply served, and that accordingly the State ought in all events to refrain from meddling in economic concerns. This notion was never in any place or time followed out to the full in practice; and hardly anyone continues to believe in it now. For it is obvious that, whatever may have been the situation a century ago, to-day the absence of State intervention does not lead to this supposedly beneficent competition. On the contrary, in nearly all the key industries and services, what happens in the absence of State intervention is not free competition, but some form of monopoly. Not all industries are monopolistic in structure; but there is hardly one left that is not monopolistic at some stage. Even where competition survives between the makers of finished goods, the producers of the materials out of which these goods are made may form a powerful monopoly. Finance—the provision of credit to the producers—is almost everywhere a highly monopolistic affair; and even where monopoly is incomplete huge concerns in many cases so dominate the market that it is a mockery to speak of free competition. Wages, too, are regulated more and more by large-scale collective bargains between Trade Unions and associations of employers, and the selling prices of goods are often fixed by the manufacturer, so that one retailer may not undercut another, even if he wishes to do so. The absence of State intervention no longer means competition as the dominant characteristic of the economic world: it means regulation by irresponsible monopolies instead of regulation in the common interest.

This would not suffice to condemn the system, if these monopolies did in fact serve the public well. But the natural tendency is for most monopolists, and most combines aiming at monopoly, to live in perpetual fear of glutting the market. The aim of those who control them is to make as much profit as possible; and this *must* be their aim, as matters stand, for unless they make it so they will speedily go to the wall. The highest profit is in most cases to be won, or seems likeliest to be won, not by producing as much as possible, but, on the contrary, by limiting production to what can be sold at a fairly high price. There are exceptions to this rule, in the case of goods the demand for which can be expanded considerably even by a small reduction in price; for in such a situation it may suit the monopolist to increase his output. It suited Ford to produce a very large number of motor-cars, in order to secure the full economy of mass-production. But such instances are exceptional. Much oftener, what happens is that the business concerns turn out many fewer goods than they could, with the consequence that many workers are left unemployed and have to look to the State for support.

This is so much a commonplace that a great many people have become accustomed to it, and regard it as quite natural that millions of people should be out of work when they themselves, and millions of others, are going short of the things they could make. Yet such a state of affairs is, when you come to think of it, plainly immoral and absurd. If the means of making things exist, and the things are needed to give people a decent standard of life, it is manifestly wrong not to make them; and any economic system which leads to such results stands condemned at the bar of morality and commonsense. It is, no doubt, *possible* that men are so incompetent at managing their affairs as to be incapable of doing any better. But they ought to try; and the method most widely advocated of curing this evil is that of Socialism.

At this point, it used always to be answered that Socialism was no doubt a very beautiful and lofty ideal, but could not be made to work in practice. 'Human nature', we were told, made it impossible. That argument is now out of court. For Socialism *has* worked, over a period of more than two decades, in one of the largest countries in the world. The system which was set up in 1917 in the Soviet Union has many faults; but it has banished unemployment and set out to produce goods up to the very limit of its productive power. It used to be said that a Socialist State would inevitably break down because its citizens would insist on consuming all they could produce, instead of setting aside adequate provision for the accumulation of new productive power. That argument also is out of court; for the Soviet Union has put into capital accumulation probably a larger proportion of its national income than has ever been put by any capitalist State—and that despite the necessity it has been under of spending vast sums on armaments in self-defence.

It can no longer be argued that Socialism is unworkable. But it can, of course, still be held to be undesirable. There, the favourite contention is that Socialism is destructive of the freedom of the common man. That is harder to answer; for the situation in Russia in respect of freedom is much less obvious. I have listened to many inconclusive arguments about the relative extent of freedom in Russia and in Great Britain. One side will stress the suppression of doctrines supposed to make against the security of the Soviet State, the insistence on Marxian orthodoxy as the basis of all thinking, the prosecution of 'comrades' who are held to have deviated from the true faith. The other side will argue that the Soviet workmen, conscious of owning the factories they work in and the State itself, emancipated from subservience to persons of a higher social class, much more able to live private lives after their chosen fashion than most people in a class-ridden society, enjoy a much larger real freedom than the workers in capitalist countries. In effect, each side puts the accent on certain particular aspects of freedom, and ignores other aspects. They are both right, and they are both wrong. However, the fact that the argument remains inconclusive does show that social control of the State and the means of production is not by itself enough to ensure freedom in all its desirable forms. The Soviet Union is not a free democracy, as we understand the term; but then—neither is Great Britain, as they understand it.

This suggests that there is a real danger, if we concentrate on securing the equal chance for all and the basic standard of living for all, to the exclusion of the type of democratic freedom which I have discussed earlier in this chapter, of our getting into conflict with a tradition of free speech and free organisation which hardly existed in Russia, but is very powerful here. Each country, in amending its social institutions, has to build upon its own past. Soviet Communism in Russia is what it is, in many respects, because Czardom was what it was; and

British Socialism, when and if it comes to power, will have on it the stamp of the British tradition. That is why it is foolish for Communists to call upon us to do just as the Russians did. Our circumstances are so different that our revolution, when it comes, will necessarily take a different form and lead to a different set of institutions. The kinds of freedom we value and enjoy now we must carry over into the new society we mean to build; and we must add to them other kinds of freedom which are now denied to most of our people.

I have no wish to make light of the danger which threatens the kind of democratic freedom that I value. But I maintain that this danger arises, not from Socialism, but from the underlying conditions which make Socialism a necessity. I have tried to describe how capitalism, turning from competition to monopoly, refuses to use the growing powers of production for fear of losing profit. It forms vast aggregations of capital, and the controllers of these exercise immense coercive power over the lives of men. There is no way of curbing this anti-social power except by bringing these great monopolies under social control. But to do this is not, I agree, to remove the danger of their trampling the individual underfoot. For the danger arises out of their hugeness, however they are controlled; and this hugeness is an inescapable characteristic of the modern way of living. It is a direct outcome of the advance of science, of the growth of population, and of the development of urban forms which has accompanied these changes.

We shall not get rid of this danger by rejecting Socialism. Indeed, what will happen to us is that we shall get Fascism instead, as the only political instrument powerful enough to keep capitalism in being. For the monopolists, unless we take them over, will resort to Fascism as a means of holding us in subjection. It is a plain truth, as Marx pointed out long ago, that the development of productive technique presses on continuously towards a growing 'socialisation', in the sense that all economic processes become increasingly interdependent. The culmination of this development is complete unification of control; but it remains an open question whether this control is to be exercised by and on behalf of the whole people or by a gang which succeeds in imposing its rule on the entire society. Socialism is one form of this process of 'socialisation': Fascism is the other. There is no third alternative consistent with the requirements of modern economic technique.

If we wish to repel Fascism, we must achieve Socialism. But we are free to give Socialism the shape that best suits our wills. Within the inevitable hugeness of the modern social structure, we are free to set up democratic institutions designed to counteract this hugeness, by providing ample means for the expression of diversity and for free association among groups of men. These opportunities must be provided within the framework of hugeness; for if we try to run counter to the tendencies of scientific advance we shall assuredly fail. The hugeness does offer us the means of ensuring to every person in our community a decent standard of national living; and this boon is out of our reach on any other terms. This is an overriding condition: our task is, having accepted it, to render it compatible with the claims of democratic freedom.

With this in mind, let us consider more closely, in terms of the economic structure of our society, what it implies. The old Socialist slogan, we have seen, proclaimed the need for socialising 'the means of production, distribution and exchange'. We have to ask how far this is really necessary in order to establish communal control over the working of the economic system, to ensure the full use of the productive powers, or to establish justice in the distribution of the social product.

Why do we want to socialise any industry or service? For one or both of two reasons. Because it is working badly or inefficiently under private ownership, and is failing to give either the consumers generally or the producers whom it employs a square deal; or because it places too much power in the hands of its private owners, and enables them to use this power for anti-social ends. Let me take two obvious cases as a first, incomplete illustration of what I mean. The coal industry manifestly ought to be socialised because under private control it has failed either to provide reasonably cheap coal for the consumers, or to keep the miners busy, or to pay those whom it has employed a decent wage. The economies that could be achieved by running the coal industry as a unified service are very great, and have been explained over and over again. Common pumping arrangements, the removal of barrier coal between separate pits, pooling of pits into larger units, common marketing and systematic development of new coal-bearing areas—all these offer large opportunities which could be taken if control were unified. But unification must be under social ownership, because in private hands it would mean a much too powerful monopoly.

For our other preliminary example, take the newspaper trade. Here the question is not mainly one of inefficiency, but of anti-social power. Of late years, a few great syndicates have swallowed up paper after paper. The independent local press has been totally extinguished in many areas; and new competition has been rendered nearly impossible by the vast capital which is necessary. Consequently, a very few men wield an immense power in spreading or suppressing or distorting news and in manipulating public opinion. Either they do this for their own political ends, or purely for profit, or from a mixture of these motives. In any event, the result is evil. It is plainly wrong and undesirable for these vast powers to be wielded irresponsibly by rich men, or for newspapers to be conducted solely on the basis of extracting the largest possible profit. Newspapers ought to be organs of opinion as well as of news. They ought to be so organised as to make possible the expression of a wide diversity of opinion, and not to repeat through a megaphone the views of a narrow group of very rich men.

This case, admittedly, is very much harder than that of the coal mines. Coal needs producing and marketing efficiently, with good conditions for the miners; and that is all. News and opinion cannot be satisfactorily marketed by the ton like coal. We do not want a 'unified' newspaper industry with all the papers repeating the same thing, even if what they repeat is dictated by men who are responsible to the public and believe that they are speaking for the public advantage. Accordingly, I do not suggest that all newspapers ought to be run by the State. What is needed is, rather, a common distributive machinery, common agencies for expensive news-gathering, and, I think, communally-owned presses which could be rented by groups desiring to produce a paper. The vital thing here is to reduce the minimum cost of starting a newspaper, so as to abolish the monopoly of the very rich.

I have taken this difficult case, rather than an easier one, because it so well illustrates the dilemma into which we are forced by the growth in the scale of production. To leave newspapers to 'private enterprise' does not mean that we have, or can have, a free democratic press. It means a press dominated by a few millionaires. On the other hand, socialisation would involve the risk of having only a Government press, with no opportunity for the expression of varying views or the publication of news unwelcome to the Government. We have therefore to find a mean—to eliminate millionaire control without substituting another form of unfreedom.

The case for socialisation, as I have stated it so far, is incomplete. Let us go back to our example of the coal mines. It is all very well to say that we must get the mines so controlled that they are able to employ all the miners and produce as much coal as possible. Mere socialisation of the mining industry cannot lead to that result, because it is useless to produce more coal than can find a market. The market for coal is only in part a consumers' market. If we give everyone a decent living income, more coal will be used both in household grates and in making gas and electricity for private consumption, and also in other ways. But a large part of the market for coal lies in the demand of other industries, such as steel-making. If we allow the steel industry to be controlled by a private monopoly, which proceeds to restrict the output of steel in order to keep prices and profits high, there will be unemployed miners, even if the mining industry is in the hands of a public body.

In effect, socialisation is not a matter of this or that industry, considered apart from others, but of the general driving force behind the economic system as a whole. That is where the more progressive Liberals are apt to make a great mistake. They profess themselves ready to consider, on the merits of the particular case, the socialisation of any industry which is being inefficiently run. But the unemployment and the underproduction which are the cause of our present economic system are not mainly a matter of inefficiency in any particular industry. They are also the result of a more general inefficiency, or anti-social quality, in the entire system. The root trouble is that industry, taken as a whole, produces not what is needed, or what it could produce, but only so much as will yield to its owners the largest possible profit. This is the disease which we have to cure; and we shall not cure it merely by transferring to public control a few industries which are exceptionally badly run.

The first principle of soundness in an economic system is that it should use all the available resources of man-power to work upon the gifts of nature up to the point at which men prefer having more leisure to having more material wealth. This principle cannot be made operative where profit, and not need, is the determining factor in production. It can be brought into effect only by a radical change of system, which will either supersede the profit motive altogether, or relegate it to a secondary place. It is for society as a whole, and not for any profit-seeking capitalist, to settle how much it is worth while to produce; and it is monstrous that any man should be unable to find work as long as his labour could add something worth while, from the standpoint of human wants, to the sum-total of production.

How are we to make this principle operative? Clearly by planning—that is, by deciding, collectively and responsibly, how the available man-power and instruments of production are to be used. I shall have to discuss later how, in terms of social machinery, this can best be done. My point now is that it must *be* done, if we are to make an end of poverty and unemployment, and are not to waste the great opportunities which science is putting into our hands. It cannot be done, as long as private persons are free to turn their workers on to the streets as soon as it becomes more profitable to reduce production than to maintain it, or whenever some new invention makes it possible to reduce the number of workers employed.

I am not blaming the ordinary private employer. As matters stand, he has usually no choice; for he cannot be expected to go on producing at a loss. I am not even blaming gently those who direct the great capitalist monopolies; for they too are only acting in accordance with the system that makes profit the criterion of what is to be produced. What I am saying is that the system is radically and utterly wrong, and needs to be changed, not merely here and there, but as a whole.

What is necessary in order to change it? Before answering that question, let us look at what happens in the Soviet Union, where it has been radically changed. We can then see better, not how to imitate Russia, but how to apply the lessons of Russia to our own considerably different case.

In the Soviet Union, production proceeds according to a Five Years Plan. This plan is drawn up by a public body, which works upon lesser plans drawn up by the numerous bodies through which the plan as a whole will have to be carried into effect. The plan is, essentially, a plan for using all the available resources in order to produce as many as possible of the goods and services needed by the citizens of the Soviet Union. It is a plan for turning out these goods in the best possible proportions, both between different sorts of consumers' goods and between such goods on the one hand, and on the other machinery for the production of future goods. The first question asked in making up the plan is not 'Will it *pay* to produce these goods?' but 'Are they needed?' or rather, 'Where so many things are needed, what needs ought to come first?' On this basis there is never any question of saying that some of the available workers are not worth using; for plainly every able-bodied person is worth using where so many needs have to go unsatisfied. Unemployment, save as a quite minor incident of changing jobs, simply disappears. If the Soviet Union is still poor, that is because it started very poor, and not because it is not abolishing poverty as fast as it can.

Naturally, Soviet planning does not work with perfect efficiency. All manner of things go wrong and have to be put right. The plan is being continually modified throughout the period of its execution. It is not a rigid scheme, but something to aim at, and to amend wherever it is shown to have been wrongly drawn. Nor is it all rigidly centralised. There are planning authorities in each separate Republic of the Soviet Union and in each city. Each successive plan has shown a greater amount of decentralisation—a handing over of more responsibility to the smaller planning units. Only for a very few industries is the plan centrally administered: in most cases, all the centre does is to act as a co-ordinator of local or sectional plans. The aim is to diffuse responsibility, not to concentrate it. The more people can be given responsibility for the plan and for its execution, the better will its democratic basis be assured.

Now, when this process of planning was started, most of the experts, including most economists, said flatly that it would never work. Some of them maintained that it would break down because of its top-heaviness, and because an organisation so gigantic was quite past the power of men to control. Others, especially among the professional economists, were so affrighted at the very notion of producing anything except under the stimulus of the profit motive that they simply announced that a system so different from that about which they had been teaching their pupils could not possibly exist, and awaited with daily impatience the news of Soviet collapse. But the Russian system did not collapse: it worked. The very mistakes which were made—and there were plenty of them—demonstrated its strength; for it was able to retrieve them, and to go on swiftly to fresh ventures. It was proved beyond a doubt that it was possible for a great country, not merely to discard the profit motive as the spur to production without disaster, but to advance without it in industrial efficiency very much faster than any other country had ever advanced before.

I am writing this book at a moment when even the critics who have been maintaining for years past, in face of all the facts, that these victories of Soviet planning were unreal have been silenced by the magnificent resistance of the Soviet forces to the sudden and treacherous attack of the Nazi power. Whatever may be the outcome of this struggle, the Russians have already done amply enough to prove the virtues of Socialist planning. No bravery of their soldiers could have availed to check the Nazi advance if there had not been at its back an impressive industrial effort; and this effort, be it remembered, was achieved in less than a generation, in a backward country terribly short of technicians and skilled workers, practically without external aid. It was achieved by Socialist planning, which had released the pent-up energies of the people, instead of suffering them to be held back by fear of 'spoiling the market'.

This Soviet planning has rested throughout on the public ownership and control of all the large-scale industries, of the transport system, of power supply, of banking and finance, and of all foreign trade. It has rested, for some time past, on a collective system in agriculture more akin to Co-operation than to State Collectivism. In small-scale industry, it has rested on a form of Co-operation among the working craftsmen —the *artel*; and in distribution on a mixture of State, Co-operative and producers' enterprise. It is not a uniform structure, nor is it fixed. Changes are continually being made in it; and its completed form cannot yet be discerned. But there is no doubt about its essential character, which is that the key industries and services, on which the rest depend, are firmly controlled, and their output planned, in accordance with a collective conception of needs. From one Five Years Plan to another the emphasis changes. The heavy industries, agriculture, transport, the consumers' trades, each in turn come into the centre of the picture. This happens, not by accident or by the 'higgling' of the market, but because it is thought to be right from the standpoint of the community as a whole.

The institution of Socialist planning in the Soviet Union followed upon a revolution, which was itself the sequel to a nearly complete collapse of the preceding social order. In the course of the war and the revolution, Russian industry had gone entirely to pieces: output was down to a few per cent. of what it had been in 1913. The Soviet planners had to start almost from nothing, building up a totally new economic system. That was in a sense an advantage in the long run, for it enabled them to start clean. But it meant terrible suffering while the new order was being created. It also meant much more centralisation of control than would have been necessary if the planners had been taking over a going concern. The planning had to begin from the centre, and decentralisation had to be introduced gradually as the regional organisations grew strong enough to take responsibility upon themselves. This process of diffusing responsibility is still going on. It is an essential part of what the planners have in mind.

Our circumstances in Great Britain are very different from those in Russia in 1917. We have, in comparison with the Soviet Union, an abundance of skilled workers, trained technicians, and competent administrators. Our economic system is working, even if it is not working well. The blows of war, so far from shattering it, have strengthened it, and have enforced the introduction of co-ordinating controls which were missing from it before. We have begun to plan—for planning is an imperative necessity in time of war; and war has banished unemployment for the time, and caused us to produce more nearly up to the limits of our capacity. It is true that we are not yet producing as much as we could produce—not by a long way. We have resorted to planning reluctantly and half-heartedly, and without getting rid of the vested interests, which are still everywhere hampering the work of organisation. We have, however, made big advances since our national peril became plain and compelled us to take reorganisation seriously in hand. We do now possess the rudiments of a system of planning which can, if we so decide, be applied to the uses of peace as well as war.

Moreover, a curious thing has happened. Although our planners have done their level best to leave the profit system undisturbed, by continuing to allow private firms to make contracts with the Government instead of taking over the factories and producing whatever is needed without any question of profit—in spite of this, the profit motive has partly ceased to work. It has been impossible not to limit profits—for the failure to do this would have caused too dangerous an outcry; but the consequences of taxing away the excess is that in all the trades which are busy on war work almost every employer is making much more profit than he is allowed to retain; so that it hardly matters at all to him whether his books show a larger or a smaller profit at the end of the year. The consequence is that a great many employers can hardly be said to-day to be working in any sense under the stimulus of the profit motive. Their conduct is guided, not by the hope of making larger profits, but by their will to help in the national effort for victory in the war. I have talked to many of them; and I know that they find this situation very strange. Having been brought up to believe in profit as the sole spur to productive efficiency, they now find themselves spurred on by a quite different motive. They are bewildered; and in many instances the result is a strange confusion in their economic ideas and an opening of their minds to the possibility of an alternative economic system which they would have rejected as utterly impracticable only a year or two ago.

I do not suggest that this is true of all employers, or of the majority. But I think it is true of quite a number, and that it should be so is an exceedingly hopeful sign. For if we are to make the transition to a new industrial system without the chaos and suffering which the Russians had to undergo, it is of vital importance that we should carry with us as many as possible of the men who know how to run industry, and should not have to find and train a totally fresh team.

I think this change of attitude is a great deal commoner

among small and middle-sized employers than among those who are at the head of great monopolistic concerns. Naturally so; for the great monopolists have been so used to following anti-social policies and pitting their interests against those of the community that their capitalist sentiments are far more ingrained. They have also much more to lose, in power as well as riches. The ordinary employer may be as well or better placed as manager of a business run in the public interest and under public control as if he has to face the task of finding markets for himself when the war is over—to say nothing of the danger that one or another of the big combines may set to work to crush him out. On the other hand, the big monopolist does not want to work for the public. He loves power, for himself. Nine times out of ten he is by temperament a robber-baron, and not a technician or a business manager. He hates the thought of the State controlling him—unless it be such a State as he can himself control.

Side by side with the employers, great and small, are the salaried technicians and managers, who have been accustomed to working as the servants of capital, and trying to make as big profits as possible for their masters. These men, too, are going through a strange experience; for they also find themselves working now, not mainly for profit, but for the national cause. They are affected in much the same way as the smaller employers, having their eyes half-opened to the practicability of a different economic system, and rather bewildered by their experience. They, even more than many of the employers, are key men upon whom the efficiency of production directly depends; and in their case, unless they are very high up and in receipt of very large salaries or shares in profits, they have no valid reason for supposing that they would be worse off, in a material sense, if industry were brought under public ownership and run in the public interest. Their opposite numbers in the Soviet Union get salaries which, allowing for differences in the wealth of the two countries, are comparable to theirs. Socialism has not meant, in practice, equality of incomes—far from it. As practised in the Soviet Union, it has meant the cancellation of unearned incomes, but not the reduction of all earners to a level.

Indeed, the technician and the manager can find much to attract them in industry run in accordance with the principles of Socialist planning. Which of them would not prefer to have his factory always running to capacity, with an assured market for all he could produce? This has been the position of his Russian equivalent ever since Soviet planning settled down after the initial disorder; and it is manifestly a state of things that gives the best of opportunities for doing a good job of work.

Nevertheless, many of the technicians and managers feel a great reluctance to accept Socialism. This is partly because they have been accustomed to regard themselves as belonging to the side of 'Capital' rather than 'Labour', and as members of a superior class; and also partly because they feel a mistrust of 'Trade Union control'. Nor is either of these feelings unnatural. In a society still ridden by the profit motive, and worshipping riches as a sign of achievement and prestige, anyone who is raised in income above the common level is under a temptation to ally himself in spirit with his 'betters' against those who are worse off and may, therefore, envy him and wish to pull him down. Moreover, in such a society, the Trade Unions, excluded from any positive share in the conduct of industry, are compelled to defend their members' interests largely in negative and restrictive ways. From the standpoint of the technician or the manager, they are always obstructively objecting to things he reasonably wants to do; and he is apt to fear that under a Socialist system their power to obstruct will be greatly increased. I believe this view to be the very reverse of the truth, and to have been proved so in Russia. For under Socialism the Trade Union becomes the constructive ally of management both in improving the efficiency of production and in lightening the workers' tasks. No longer afraid of being exploited by the profit-seekers, the workers become interested in the efficiency of the factories in which they work, and eager to play their part in the common service.

The 'team spirit', which many capitalist firms use all sorts of devices for vamping up, develops naturally; and managers and workers become partners instead of antagonists. Frictions no doubt still arise; but there is no longer the underlying class-hostility which magnifies small grievances into matters of principle and makes mountains out of molehills, to the torment of the manager who is trying to do his best.

The upshot of this discussion is that war conditions, by limiting the operation of the profit motive, have done an important work of psychological preparation for change among employers and managers alike. The other side of the medal is that they have also strengthened the position of the great combines as against the smaller firms, because these combines have largely been allowed to turn themselves into 'Controls' acting on behalf of the State and wielding the State's authority. Where this has happened, the profit motive has *not* ceased to operate. For the great capitalists, having larger incomes than they know what to do with, are in general more interested in future than in present profits. They want capital appreciation rather than income as a tribute to their power; and they cannot keep themselves from scheming now with a view to strengthening their post-war position. This often causes them to hamper the war effort, because they are dominated by a fear of 'excess capacity' in the industries they control, and therefore unwilling to expand production during the war, even when expansion is needed to the utmost. Such men are hardly open to conversion to belief in an economic order which would knock away the foundations of their power. They remain 'public enemies', even when they are quite unconscious that they are acting anti-socially.

To them it is of little use to appeal for a change of vision. But it is of use to appeal to the employer or to the salaried manager or technician whose heart is in doing his job well. Such men want to know—at least, many of them are reaching that point—how exactly industry would work under Socialism, and what exactly the Socialists do propose. In the next chapter I shall do my best to tell them, and at the same time to explain to others the essentials of the immediate Socialist programme, both for winning the war and for the reconstruction that is to follow it, as far as relates to the ownership and control of industry and commerce and finance. When we have got the gist of that programme clearly into our minds, we can go on to consider what are the forces making for its achievement, and how they can best be organised so as to make the transition as painless and easy as it can be made.

III

PROGRAMME FOR INDUSTRY

I HAVE no intention of supplying in this chapter the blue prints for a Socialist industrial system. For those readers who want a fuller version of the proposals which I am here merely outlining, there is a book of mine, called *A Plan for Democratic Britain*, in which I have tried to set down the essentials of an immediate Socialist policy. This book was published a few months before the outbreak of war, and if I were writing it now I should put many things in it rather differently. The war has changed many things and, in especial, has made the need for Socialism much more urgent and the likelihood of its speedy advent considerably greater. But the main features of Socialist policy have not been very much affected, as far as the future is concerned. Temporary problems of 'War Socialism' have arisen, and have to be solved quickly if we are to muster up all our forces for the defeat of Nazism. But, in relation to the period after the war, all that has happened is that the dissolution of the capitalist order has been brought a great deal nearer, so that we shall need to be speedier and more thorough in the application of Socialist remedies. The essential Socialist case remains pretty much as it was: the problems of running industry as a public service and replacing the profit motive by other, less anti-social, incentives remain practically unchanged. The differences are, first, that the conditions of warfare have given us a new starting point by thrusting the profit motive and the question of unemployment temporarily into the background, and that the destruction of the pre-war system on the continent, being much more thorough than what has happened here, involves a more thoroughgoing reconstruction than most Socialists have hitherto contemplated, and affords therewith larger opportunities for the building of an international Socialist order.

In this chapter I shall begin with certain immediate problems arising directly out of the needs of war. I shall try to show how a more socialistic policy here and now could improve the quality of the war effort and achieve a fuller mobilisation of our resources for the tasks of victory. Having done this, I shall come to the questions of reconstruction and try to suggest how much Socialism we shall need as a minimum basis for setting about the rebuilding of Britain on satisfactory, democratic lines.

Great Britain's war effort up to the present time has been a curious blend of muddle and miracle, of devoted service and of blind refusal to face facts. We went into the war under the Chamberlain Government with 'Trust private enterprise' as the official slogan. Where 'Controls' were plainly necessary, they were put for the most part into the hands of the leaders of big business. That is to say, the very persons who had, for years past, been bending all their energies to destroying 'redundant capacity' and restricting output in order to maintain profits were entrusted with the task of raising output to the highest possible level in order to meet the needs of war. At the same time, orders went forth that there was to be as little interference as possible with the affairs of private firms, or with the methods of collective bargaining between employers' associations and Trade Unions, or with the normal working of trade in home or foreign markets. There was, of course, a big increase in the volume of Government orders, and many new firms began to work for the State either directly or, more often, as sub-contractors for the regular suppliers of the public departments. But there was no realisation at all, even in face of the complete mobilisation of German industry which had been carried through long before the war, of the need for any real plan of war production or of the necessity for throwing every ounce of available economic energy into the war effort.

The results were disastrous. When France collapsed in the early summer of 1940 and the relatively small British army which had been sent to the continent lost nearly all its stores and equipment, there was nothing to replace those losses. We had the men, but we had no arms; and employers who could have been turning out vital munitions of war were even then still being incited to export as much machinery and similar goods as possible, in order to ease the strain on our foreign exchange. If Hitler had invaded Great Britain in the summer of 1940, he would have found almost nothing in his way, once he had been able to rush his armies across the narrow seas.

Thereafter did come a great change. During the next few months employers and workers alike 'went to it' with a will, and miracles were wrought in the way of hard, continuous labour and increased immediate production. But this remarkable effort, splendid as it was, was a piece of improvisation. There was still no plan behind it: nor was a great deal done towards making a plan, though it was plain to anyone with a grain of commonsense that the effort could not continue for more than a very short time in its existing form. The strain of it was wearing everybody out, and there was a serious danger of collapse out of sheer exhaustion not many months ahead.

Yet effective planning still hung fire for a variety of reasons. The greatest of these was that any effective plan involved a much greater interference with private business than even the new Churchill Government was prepared to insist on. If the production of munitions was to be speeded up to the full and the home consumers' market to be kept at the same time supplied with what was really essential, there plainly had to be both a drastic rationalisation, or 'concentration', of the less essential industries and trades, in order to release workers, machinery and factory space for more urgent tasks, and also, in the trades which were expanding on war work, a parallel rationalisation designed to secure the fullest and most effective use of scarce kinds of skill, scarce machine-tools and other equipment, and scarce managerial and technical ability. There had also to be a clearly defined system of 'priorities', both for imports and in the use of scarce materials and transport space. And, with these things, there had to be a control of consumers' expenditure, in order to bring about as fair as possible a distribution of the restricted supplies of ordinary goods.

Little by little some of these things were done. But what was done was done hesitantly, and by small stages; and many of the most necessary things were hardly done at all. Many of them remain undone even now, after more than three years of war. The 'concentration' of the less essential industries was for some time applied only to a very few trades, and then half-heartedly. The rationalisation of the war industries was hardly attempted at all, save to a small extent by tidying up the methods of placing sub-contracts. There was still, strange to relate, right up to 1942 no clearly conceived system of priorities, and the supply departments even now, despite the institution of a Ministry of Production, scramble one with another for essential materials and machines. As for consumers' expenditure, rationing has been extended to cover clothing and a number of additional kinds of food; but in a good many respects consumers are still left to scramble for the limited supplies, so that naturally the rich mostly come off a great deal better than the poor, and the idlers than those who are too busy to flit from shop to shop. Wages remain an unregulated chaos, so that legend is free to exaggerate the earnings of the munition workers and spread discontent among the conscripts who are serving on army pay. Recruiting is a muddle, so that the taking of too many miners into the forces threatens the country with a dangerous shortage of coal. There is discontent in the factories, on account, not of overwork, but of waiting about with nothing to do because materials have failed to arrive, or the design of a plane or a tank has been suddenly changed. Employers still curse the departments which keep them hanging about in corridors, or scurrying to and fro in endless searches for the official whose business it is to give this or that authorisation, or set some blunder right.

Be it admitted that some of this confusion is unavoidable. The same sort of thing probably happens in Germany—let us hope it does. But a great deal of it is not unavoidable, but is the result of a deliberate refusal to organise the country for totalitarian war. No one, at any rate no Englishman, likes being organised on totalitarian lines. But war is a question, not of liking, but of necessity. And I am sure there are very many among both employers and workers to-day who would prefer being given straight orders to being bandied about and left with a sense that their services are being only half-used or used without the guidance of any clearly conceived plan. I do not mean that I want, as some martinets do, to rush the whole nation under military discipline. Far from it. No such thing is necessary or desirable. But I do want, up top, a definite plan of production, and I do want every factory, every employer, technician and manager, and every workman to have a defined place in that plan, and be told to go where he, or it, is most urgently wanted.

Begin with the factories, which are largely the key to the whole problem. Where is the sense of first allowing firms to make excess profits, and then trying to take them away by taxation? Surely it would be much more sensible for the State to take over all the factories it wants, pay a fixed rent for their use, and take the managers and technicians into direct public employment. If this were done, a number of highly desirable consequences would follow. Instead of each factory being treated as a separate business, or grouped only with other factories belonging to the same firm, factories could be arranged in the groups most convenient for war production, managers of high ability could be promoted to take charge of key groups; workers and, where necessary, machines could be shifted from factory to factory without any complications; wages and conditions could be standardised over wide areas; patents could be effectively pooled; and much better arrangements could be made for the continuous running of valuable machinery and the avoidance of 'bottle-necks' in production. These changes would lead to a large increase in output, and to much more certain prediction of the future flow of supplies.

It is true that this system would, in the businesses that were taken over, entirely eliminate the profit motive for the time being. But, as we saw in the last chapter, this motive is already largely in suspense; and, where it is still working, it is acting against the war effort and not on its side. The profit motive now, in the war trades, acts only in such a way as to cause employers to think about the effect of what they do at present on profits *after the war*; but that is not what we want them to think about, and action prompted by such thoughts hampers the war effort. We shall not lose but gain by completing the elimination of the profit motive in the war industries.

The non-war industries, which are undergoing contraction, offer a much more difficult problem. In the war industries, whatever may happen after the war, there is plenty to be done for the present. But in other industries and trades there are many who are facing the prospect of ruin here and now. In the 'concentration' industries there has been provision for some sort of compensation by means of pooling arrangements for firms which are compelled to close down; but these arrangements are threatened with breakdown as reconcentration further reduces the number of firms able to remain in production. No doubt a number of the closed firms can, in one way or another, shift over to war work. Their worry, especially that of the smaller employers, is mainly about what is to happen to them after the war; for many of them feel doubtful whether they will ever be in a position to reopen their works. But in many trades it is practically impossible to change over, and the hardship is serious. Moreover, in other occupations there are many who are even worse off—shopkeepers, unable to keep their shops open and with no prospect of compensation for the loss of their means of life; very small firms, unable to retain even the minimum nucleus of labour needed for keeping at work or to find anyone who will enter into a pooling arrangement with them; businesses ruined by the evacuation of population from defence areas, or by the *blitz*. There is no plan for people of these sorts, except to tell them that they must do the best they can, and will receive relief if they become really destitute.

Now, this sort of case presents a real difficulty—especially in the distributive trades. From the standpoint of commonsense there *are* too many small shops, and their existence involves a great waste of man-power and capital. Some small productive businesses are highly efficient; but many are not, and were, in fact, in process of being squeezed out by the big producers quite apart from the war. It is not good sense or consistent with our will to end poverty by using our resources better, to hold out hopes that all the displaced little businesses will be able to start up again after the war. But—and here is the point—it is quite intolerable to the small man to be told this unless it is also made quite clear to him that we are *not* going back after the war to an economic system which allows widespread unemployment to exist, rests on no plan, and, because of this, encourages him to set up his little shop or workshop as a way of escape from the dole or from the precarious existence of wage-earning. No doubt his position as small shopkeeper or workshop master has also been highly precarious; but it has offered compensations. If it had not, the number of shopkeepers in South Wales would not have increased all through the depression, though the local population was declining fast, and its purchasing power faster still.

It is dishonest to hold out to all these 'little men' the hope that everything will be all right again after the war. It will not, if being 'all right' means returning to their pre-war way of living, which was in fact, for many of them, poor and uncertain to a degree. It ought not to be 'all right' in this sense; for their pre-war way of living was, for many of them, uneconomic both in a personal sense and from the standpoint of the community. Their future ought to lie, not in a return to their little businesses, irrespective of their efficiency, but in many of them being found, according to their skill and capacities, alternative ways of earning their living and serving the public interest. What is utterly unfair is, without any such promise for the future, to turn them out now, without any such compensation as is readily given to employers in a larger way of business.

If it would be right, in the war trades, to cut out the profit motive altogether and put every employer and manager on a public salary (and every worker on a public wage), would it not be the sensible course, for the war period, to put everybody on a fixed income? I quite realise that this involves enormous complications. What is to happen to the man who has to pay rent for a big house, or who is committed to large payments for life insurance, or house purchase, or for the education of his children? Is the servant-keeping class to be reduced to doing all its own housework, in houses built on the assumption that menial labour will be forthcoming when it is wanted? Are ladies and gentlemen to cease being ladies and gentlemen, for the duration of the war, whatever may be in store for them afterwards?

No. I am not suggesting that. I have, indeed, no use for ladies and gentlemen, if the phrase means persons who claim to live expensively at the cost of the community without doing any work. But equally I do not believe it to be practicable, or for the present desirable, to equalise incomes for all. I have no objection to a Town Clerk, or a skilled manager, getting up to, say, two or even three thousand a year, provided that he works for it in accordance with the magnitude of his reward. Moreover, I recognise that people who have been accustomed, as property owners, to drawing incomes for doing nothing, had better not be suddenly and completely deprived of them. To do this, except in the course of a revolution, would be to create a sense of hardship and actually to inflict much unnecessary suffering. For the time being, unearned incomes must go on, because they are part of the very foundations of our society, and we cannot afford to rebuild society from the foundations in the middle of a war.

This does not mean that we need leave matters as they are. It is practicable to limit unearned incomes, though not to abolish them; and it is also practicable to offer a living income to everyone who has lost his normal means of living, on the sole condition that he is prepared to hold himself at the State's disposal, to work where, and at what, he is needed most. It is practicable to put the 'small man' who is displaced on the same basis for compensation as the larger employer, even if it is not possible to promise that he shall have his business back intact when the war is over.

Taxation is a bad way of limiting incomes. When it takes the form of taxes on excess profits, it is impossible to make the general public believe in it, even if the rate is raised to 100 per cent. All sorts of questions arise about how much a man may charge up as 'business expenses', and how much he can tuck away in the form of hidden additions to capital. When it is a matter of taxing private incomes, as distinct from business profits, the incidence is much clearer. But, even so, the question remains, Why not avoid the distribution of incomes beyond what is needed to prevent hardship, instead of taxing the surplus after it has been paid out? There will never be a rational wage policy until other incomes are brought under effective regulation. No man, during the war, ought to have a larger income than he really needs, taking his commitments into account; and, if we want to prevent the 'vicious spiral' of wages and prices, this is the conclusion to which we shall have to come.

As for labour, there is no need for putting it under military discipline, or for other measures of a similar sort urged by the militarily-minded. Put industry under public ownership for the war period, on the lines which I have suggested, and the problem of transferring labour to where it is wanted becomes relatively simple—as simple as transferring a Post Office worker from one district to another. What is wrong is to expect the workman to have the feeling that he is working for the community when he continues to get his wage-packet from a private employer, just as he did in time of peace, and to be liable to be sacked, or fined, by the firm's authority, and not the State's. The Government has introduced little instalments of public employment in the special schemes it has made for mobile squads of dockers, builders, and skilled engineers. But these are on a small scale, and remain in an environment of ordinary wage-relationships between workers and private firms. At a time when the industrial worker is fully as much in the fighting line as the soldier, this is absurd. But the worker cannot be expected to accede to a discipline which is not extended to other classes as well.

I am suggesting that there is need, in order to win the war, to make large advances without further delay towards what is called 'War Socialism'. Naturally, the larger these advances are the more ready we shall be for post-war reconstruction. In 1919, after the last war, the State, incited by the profit-seekers, made great haste to abolish as quickly as possible the 'Controls' which had been created under stress of war needs, and to return to 'business as usual'. The result was seen in the criminal and disastrous boom of 1919 and 1920, when prices soared to fantastic heights and huge speculative fortunes were made, and thereafter in the great slump of 1921 and the severe difficulties from which industry never fully extricated itself right up to 1939. After this war, I feel hopeful, it will be impracticable to repeat these blunders. Whether the vested interests like it or not, the 'Controls' will have to be kept on, whatever Government is in power. Materials and shipping space will be so short that rationing of them will have to continue: the building industry will have to be publicly organised for a period of years for the repair of war damage and the reconstruction of cities and factories in the light of post-war needs; and there will have to be vast plans for training demobilised soldiers and munition workers for the jobs in which they will be needed under the new conditions.

Control will have to remain, whatever Government is in office. But the same controlling mechanism can be used to serve quite different ends. Under one type of Government, the 'Controls' could be used to consolidate the position of the great trusts and combines at the expense of the smaller employers and of the general public, and to establish a sort of 'Industrial Feudalism' under which the State would become little more than an instrument in the hands of big business and high finance. Under another type of Government, the 'Controls' could be used as instruments for the making of a new industrial order, based on planning for public service.

In the economic field, as in a theatre of war, certain positions are of special strategical importance. The side which holds them holds the key to the entire situation. In economics, the key positions, as I see the matter, are the banking system, with its control over money and the supply of credit; the fuel and power industries, which largely determine the costs and location of other manufacturing processes; transport; and the heavy industries, which produce basic raw materials, durable capital goods, and also armaments or the semi-manufactures out of which armaments are made. Whoever controls these key positions is master of the industrial system. If these industries and services can be brought under democratic control, and so organised as to serve the public interest, it will be a matter of secondary importance how other industries and services are owned or managed.

This group of key services is the chosen home of profit-seeking monopoly. The vastest concerns, the most powerful trusts and combines, are mainly to be found in it. Bring this group under direct public ownership and control; and it will be a relatively simple matter to deal with the rest.

Accordingly, a programme of immediate post-war industrial reorganisation ought to be centred upon these essential services. It is so obvious that the banks ought to be brought under public ownership and control that I am almost ashamed to spend time on arguing the case. I will be as brief as I can. In the first place, banking policy sets limits to the volume of production and employment which industry as a whole can provide. If the banks follow a deflationary line, and insist on restricting credits in order to bring prices tumbling down, nothing can avert a major industrial depression. Notice that I put this point negatively. I do not say that the banks can bring about high production or full employment merely by creating credit: I say they can prevent production and employment by not creating it. Secondly, the success of any plan of production implies the issue of credit in the appropriate amounts to the various producing agents who are to take part in the plan. Banking policy must square with production policy, or production policy cannot be carried out. Thirdly, the banks will emerge from this war as nominal owners of a huge amount of National Debt which they have created out of nothing and lent to the State. If they are left as private concerns, they will expect to be paid back. There is no earthly reason why they should be paid back. They should be nationalised, and the State should thus become the owner of a large part of its own debt. No one will suffer confiscation as a result of this. The bank shareholders' real capital will not be affected. But the power of the banks to make money at will out of nothing ought clearly to be transferred to the public. It is a most improper power to be left in the hands of private profit-making concerns.

Fuel and power supply should also be transferred completely to public ownership. First, because they are key services affecting every other industry and service, and, secondly, because they require unified control, and are therefore liable to become dangerous monopolies if they are not publicly owned. There are additional reasons. The coal industry, as we have seen, is thoroughly inefficient and needs entire reorganisation. The supply of electric power is very closely bound up both with the rebuilding of our cities and with the resettlement of industry. It needs a complete national plan, to be carried out from start to finish under public control. It is already in part publicly owned by municipalities and by the 'Grid'. It is a simple matter to complete the process and to set about creating an electric supply system able to serve every village, as well as every town, and therewith to remove one great cause of undue urban agglomeration. Gas supply needs co-ordinating with the electricity service. Petrol supply, a great user of shipping space and a potent cause of international difficulties, needs to be conducted by a responsible public authority which can take in hand the establishment of the right relation between imports and home-produced 'oil from coal'.

Inland transport, in 1939, was a chaos of unregulated competition between road and rail services. Co-ordination is plainly needed for economy and for public convenience; and only a public authority owning the railways and a large part of the road transport services can possibly bring this about.

Moreover, freight charges affect all industries, and the facilities for transport of goods and passengers are vital factors in planning the future location of our industries and the distribution of population—and therefore in the whole business of post-war building. Shipping is the chosen home of some of the worst forms of monopoly; and it would be criminal to allow the great rebuilding of the merchant marine which is bound to follow the war to fall into the hands of the private monopolists. Air transport is an essentially international service, destined to become immensely important in post-war commerce and communication. It ought to be owned publicly by a supranational authority, and should in any case be kept firmly out of private hands.

There remain the heavy industries. One reason for keeping these in the hands of the State is that they are the main source of armaments, and we neither want the armament interests to act again as hucksters of weapons over all the world nor want the State to be at the mercy of these interests in respect of its own preparedness for facing danger. Another reason is that these industries are the chief suppliers of capital goods. That means, first, that they occupy a key position in industrial planning—for they have to produce ahead the means of producing the finished goods contemplated in any production plan—and, secondly, that they also hold a key position in international trade and in the rebuilding of Europe. Yet another reason is that, as producers of semi-manufactures, such as steel and non-ferrous metals, they lend themselves very easily to monopoly because of the large capitals which are required for economic working.

This is a very summary treatment of a number of very large questions. The purpose of it is not to describe *how* these industries ought to be socialised, but by naming them to show that the bringing of the key positions of the industrial system under effective public control is not, after all, so very large a matter. If all the industries so far spoken of were socialised, and no others, the vast majority of existing businesses would still be left in private hands.

I do not suggest that *no* other industries ought to be socialised, but only that their socialisation is—with one exception—a matter of secondary importance. If this group of industries were brought under public ownership and made the focus of a national economic plan, most of the other industries would have to fall in with the plan, in all its really essential aspects.

The exception is agriculture, or rather the land, for urban land is as important as agricultural, in relation to post-war planning. Whenever Nazi bombers destroy some part of one of our cities—say London, or Southampton, or Coventry—the question arises of what we are to do about rebuilding what has been smashed down. Suppose it seems better to reserve for the future as an open space one of these areas, and to build new houses, or shops, or offices, or factories elsewhere, the owners of the site which we propose to leave open will demand compensation for it at its full building value, while the owners of the sites we propose to use instead will demand to be paid for them, in lump sums or in rents, also at building values. As a consequence, if the land is privately owned, it will be much cheaper to allow rebuilding to take place on the old sites, even if that means reinstating the old urban congestion which the bombers have given us a chance of sweeping away. But if all land were public property, no such difficulties would arise. We should be able to choose the best sites for building and to ensure that they should be used; and it would cost no more to have the open space in the middle of the city and the buildings outside it than to have the buildings in the city and the open space outside.

There will be no satisfactory rebuilding or replanning of this country if the land is left in private hands. The evils of which everyone complains—urban congestion, ribbon development, too many buildings to the acre, too few playing fields and accessible open spaces—are the fruits of private land ownership. It is urgent that this matter be tackled now; for already in our bombed areas private owners are making plans for redevelopment which runs sharply counter to the public interest. We ought not to wait until after the war to socialise the land. We ought to insist on it being done now, as a basis for the planning and rebuilding that lie before us.

Nor is the case as it affects agriculture less cogent. The trouble with British agriculture is that it is starved for lack of capital, and offers scant prospect of a decent livelihood to any farmer who has no capital at his back. If the average farm is too small for really efficient production, that is largely because few farmers can afford to stock larger units. The man of ability who takes to farming can get no scope unless he can get money behind him. Neither most landowners who hire out their land nor most who farm it themselves have enough free capital to develop it properly. The result is that the land is broken up into uneconomic units, and that even these units are ill-equipped. If the State took over the land, it could put capital into it—whatever was needed: it could give really able farmers the opportunity, either as managers or as tenants, of farming on a larger scale; and it could so raise farming standards as to make possible the payment of decent wages without charging the consumers exorbitant prices, or fostering by protection forms of cultivation—sugar beet, for example—which have no economic basis. No doubt the State might take over the land and fail to do these things. But it *could* do them, whereas under private ownership they cannot be done at all.

To this basic programme of socialisation I should wish, for the post-war period, to add one other essential thing. International trade has now become largely a matter of organised dealings between great public corporations, either owned or recognised by the various States. It will be indispensable to carry on these forms of trading for some time after the war, when there will be huge accumulated surpluses in some countries to be disposed of, and in others starving populations to be supplied. I think the right course would be to make the trade in the main basic commodities definitely a public affair, not merely for a temporary period, but as part of the general reshaping of the economic order.

Here, then, is a manageable programme of socialisation, to

which additions could be made whenever the state of disorganisation of a particular trade or industry seemed to make them necessary. What is *not* necessary is to set out on the perilous adventure of socialising everything merely for the sake of socialising it. The need is for a general framework of socialised key industries and services—a framework within which other industries and services, socialised or not, can then be made to fit. This is requisite for the successful rebuilding of our cities and industries, and for the carrying through of a policy of unrestricted production and 'full employment'. More than this is not necessary, and might well hinder the task by imposing too heavy a burden all at once on those who will have to control the change.

Who will have to control it? It would be a most deterrent thought if we had to contemplate the control being in the hands of the Civil Service; for it would be no great gain to escape from the toils of monopoly into those of red tape. The departmental machinery of the Civil Service was not made for controlling industry, and is quite unfit for the task. The ordinary British Civil Servant is honest and, within limits, competent; but he is essentially a man of routine. He is bad at taking wide responsibility, for he is trained not to take it: he is used to a system which cuts every matter of policy up into little pieces, so that no major change can be made without involving a large number of separate decisions; and he is timid, because he has usually become a Civil Servant largely for the sake of having a fixed and regular job. The ordinary, high-up Civil Servant prides himself on being a 'safe' man; but such 'safety' is not the quality that is most needed for the building of a new industrial order.

If, then, the Civil Service is not to control industry, who is to control it? I am not speaking now of the control of high policy, which is a matter for the Government itself and for such special economic organs as the Government may create for the framing and general supervision of the national economic plan, but of the administrative control within the general directives given by the planning authority. Clearly, the only suitable claimants to the exercise of this kind of control are the same men as are now doing the job for privately owned firms and combines. These alone have the requisite knowledge and training; and socialisation will mean, not sacking them, but turning them into servants of the public.

Changes, of course, will have to be made. Hide-bound disbelievers in public enterprise will have to go, and be replaced by more alert-minded men who are prepared to throw themselves energetically into the building of the new order. There will be a chance for young men to come quickly to the front, and democratic promotion, irrespective of wealth or social connection, will be fostered. Some new men will rise right from the ranks; but the main body of the new administrators will have to be drawn from the existing technical and managerial personnel.

Moreover, business operations will have to be left free from detailed political interference. It is the business of the politicians, as representing the people, to prescribe the main lines of economic policy. But no one can be expected to manage a business well if he is liable to day-to-day interference from persons who do not understand it. Managers must be removable for incompetence or for sabotage or for failure to conform to the broad requirements of the current economic plan. But, while they remain managers, they must be given a good deal of a free hand.

If they are to be given this, the general directives within which they are to work must be clearly stated and practically conceived. This means that it is of the utmost importance to equip the political leaders with a strong and competent planning organisation to advise them. The personnel of this organisation will have also to be drawn mainly from the ranks of the managers and technicians, including the technical consultants. It will have also to represent the workers; for an essential part of successful planning is to place upon the working force of industry only such tasks as it can be made able and willing to undertake. A well-staffed Planning Commission, with no executive authority, but with full power of inspection throughout industry, is a necessary part of the equipment of the new economic order. So is a better selection of Members of Parliament and Cabinet Ministers, upon whom the political responsibility must fall; but to discuss that question now would take me too far afield.

No less important is it that in the socialised industries, and indeed throughout all industry, the general body of workers should experience a radical change of status. In the socialised industries, at any rate, the workers will be no longer instruments of private profit-making, but co-partners in a public enterprise working for the good of all. But this change, though it affords a great opportunity, does not in itself suffice to give the worker a radically different attitude towards his job. For this, he has to be taken really, and not just formally, into partnership, and to be given a real voice in determining the conditions under which he is to work. The first and most obvious way of introducing this change is to set up in every establishment a Works Council (with Shop Councils also in large establishments), not as a meeting place for the rival representatives of two 'sides', but as a body representing every grade and group in the factory as partners in the common adventure of making it a success. These bodies should be quite distinct from the Trade Unions, which will be needed as much as ever to represent the workers' collective grievances and demands. They should be regarded as essentially part of the management, as necessary to the smooth and efficient working of the factory as the regular conferences of departmental heads or technical experts, and fulfilling as constructive a function.

It may be said that the Production Committees which have now been set up in most of the big war factories meet these requirements. In fact, useful as they are within their limits, they fall short in three important respects. In the first place, they do not include representatives of the technicians and managerial grades, side by side with those of the manual workers; and for this reason they are not well equipped for dealing with many of the most essential problems of production. Secondly, the rules governing their appointment, drawn up under the influence of the Trade Unions and designed to prevent their capture by 'agitators', are such as to make them much less representative than they ought to be. This applies especially to the rule which, except in the case of new establishments, requires a very long qualifying period of service before a workman becomes eligible for a place on the Production Committee. Thirdly, the rule which prevents these Committees from dealing with any matters which are regarded as falling within the province of collective bargaining between Trade Unions and Employers' Associations unduly restricts their scope. Even in spite of these limitations, the institution of Production Committees is a notable advance, and provides a foundation on which it should be possible to build in course of time a very valuable form of workshop democracy and collective control over the processes of production.

This type of workshop organisation, very much more than workers' representation on the larger governing bodies of an industry—though that may be needed too—stands for the reality underlying the demand for 'workers' control'. Without it industry cannot be permeated by the democratic spirit of service, or the worker feel that in doing his job for the community he is really free.

IV

A CHANCE FOR EVERYBODY

SEEBOHM ROWNTREE, whose earlier studies of the problem of poverty are classics, has recently added another great public service to his achievements. He has made, in his own city, York, a careful fresh survey of the income and condition of nearly every working-class household. The result of this survey, made mainly in 1935, is to show that, out of a working-class population of 53,000, exclusive of domestic servants and of working-class persons living in public institutions—that is to say, exclusive of further large groups of very poor people—no fewer than 17,000 were compelled to live at a standard which did not satisfy their basic human needs. The standard which Mr. Rowntree took was a 'poverty line' of 43s. 6d. a week *plus* rent, at 1936 prices, for a household consisting of man and wife and three children, with larger or smaller amounts allowed for larger or smaller households. He did not, in fixing this 'poverty line', inquire how these households *actually* spent their incomes: he assumed that they were spent, with perfect enlightenment and self-restraint, in the best possible way for the purpose of maintaining a decent standard of living. In his book he recognises fully that most people do not so spend their incomes, and that in practice a substantial fraction of the 10,000 other persons who were only a little above his 'poverty line' were going seriously short of some of the things that are necessary for decent and healthy living. The numbers in this group cannot be accurately measured. What the book does prove is that nearly a third of all the working-class persons in York could not, in 1935-6, by the best possible management of their family incomes, reach a decent human standard of living, and that another 20 per cent. were in serious danger of falling short of such a standard. Add to these the workers who had found refuge in public institutions, and you get a pretty picture of the standard of living in this England of ours as it was before the outbreak of war.

It may be said that this evidence relates only to a single city. That is true, and it is also true that no other city has been surveyed recently with anything approaching the same thoroughness. But York is by no means a place that is badly off, as places go; and it is highly unlikely that a survey of the entire country would yield more encouraging results. For example, the well-known Merseyside Survey, made a few years before Mr. Rowntree's, revealed a situation fully as bad; and so did the New London Survey of 1929. Readers who wish to have further information on this point can find it in *The Condition of Britain*, which I published, jointly with my wife, two years before the outbreak of war.

It can no doubt be argued that, even if real incomes were to rise sharply, social investigators would still find evidence of widespread poverty, because they would raise their standards as fast as actual conditions improved. There is something in this; but it must be borne in mind that the Rowntree standard is not arbitrary, but is based largely on conclusions arrived at by the British Medical Association about the diets necessary for maintaining health, with the addition of estimates for other necessaries and of a small surplus to be spent on the amenities of life. There is ample evidence that some expenditure that is not theoretically necessary must be included in the minimum standard, if the conclusions drawn are to be at all close to reality. For in practice households which are below the 'poverty line' will spend money on such things, even at the cost of going short of things which are necessary for health; and this means that it is requisite to allow a margin in order to ensure a minimum of physical necessaries. Some non-necessary expenditure *is* necessary, though it need not be spent on any particular thing. Calculations which ignore this need are essentially unrealistic and inhumane.

The evidence of all the numerous social surveys made in the course of the last dozen years goes to show that something like a third of the entire working-class population has been living at a standard which cannot possibly be regarded as satisfactory, or even as adequate, if we make allowance for people's habits, to maintain a healthy way of life. Nor must it be forgotten that the worst sufferers under the prevailing conditions are the members of large families. The wage system takes no account of the number of children or other dependants whom the wage-earner has to support. Large working-class households remain for long stretches of years a long way below the 'poverty line'; and many smaller households pass through a period of 'poverty', and rise above the line only when the children grow old enough to supplement the family income. Many more families pass through 'primary poverty' than suffer under it at any one time.

These facts are now widely known, and so is the evidence of malnutrition which has been accumulated by Medical Officers of Health and other experts. Sir John Orr's calculations of the sums spent on food, as compared with the sums needed for healthy living, in households of different sizes and at different income levels, lead to the same conclusion—that nearly a third of the total population is suffering in some degree from undernourishment. Dr. M'Gonigle's investigations in Stockton-on-Tees went to show that slum-clearance might in certain cases actually make the health of poor people worse: for by compelling them to spend more on housing it left them less to spend on necessary food. Comparisons between the physical condition of boys of the same age at middle-class and working-class schools show that the former are taller and heavier than the latter. Every elementary teacher who has experience of teaching in schools in poorer and better-off neighbourhoods will agree that the poorer children are inferior in both physical and intellectual development to those drawn from less impoverished homes.

Of course they are! One becomes impatient at times of the careful investigations which are made in order to prove the obvious—that people are healthier and better developed when they have enough to eat and are properly clothed and housed. Yet the proofs have to be furnished, even when the conclusions are self-evident, because nothing short of an unanswerable parade of facts will suffice to rouse the well-to-do from their complacency.

We have seen in an earlier chapter that, whereas the facts used to parade themselves, misery walking the streets where no one could help seeing it, nowadays the facts of poverty are much less obtrusive than they were even a generation ago. There are three reasons for this—the first, that the relative amount of sheer misery *has* decreased; the second, that the poor quarters of cities have become more segregated from the richer quarters; and the third, that the unemployed, and especially the long-term unemployed, have been largely concentrated in a limited number of 'depressed areas', so that persons who do not have to visit these areas do not have to see them. As a result, it is much easier now than it used to be for fairly tender-hearted people to forget all about the misery that does not force itself on their notice, and for people of ordinary toughness to become complacent about the whole matter. I remember, when I was a boy, being taken to an Anti-Sweating Exhibition, at which I heard Gilbert Chesterton speak. I remember hearing Will Crooks talk about conditions in the East End, and encountering social workers from Toynbee Hall. I remember being deeply moved by these experiences, and being able in my mind to relate what I heard to what I saw around me. I should not have been nearly so much moved if these recitals of wretchedness had been to me only travellers' tales. It is much easier for them to be no more than tales to the young people of to-day.

Yet the misery remains, even if there is less of it, and it is, much more than it was a generation ago, quite plainly preventable. Indeed, at this very moment, when we are all being rationed and have to provision this country in face of the German blockade, much of it is being prevented, simply because human labour is scarce, and men and women who had been written off as 'unemployables' are again finding jobs. There remain, of course, some 'unemployables', even in wartime; but they are many fewer than those who were dismissed as out of the running in time of peace.

The point is that we can feed these people a good deal better than they were being fed before the war, even when the nation as a whole is half cut off from its normal sources of supply. We can, moreover, feed most of them, not as a charity, public or private, but as a return for work done. In peace-time, a man or woman was 'unemployable' if no one could see a prospect of profit in employing him. To-day, though profit remains, the amount of production is determined by other forces.

So it should be, and will be, in time of peace. The most important thing we have to do in order to banish poverty is to abolish unemployment, or, to put the matter more constructively, to see that the whole country is given the chance of working right up to the point at which more leisure becomes preferable to more goods of a material kind. From the standpoint of society, a person is worth employing if he produces, not necessarily enough to pay for what he and his dependants consume, but anything at all beyond the costs, other than their consumption, which employing him, rather than not employing him, involves. He is worth employing, purely from an economic standpoint, if by producing he can make some contribution to the cost of his maintenance and that of his dependants. This is a different criterion from the human criterion, by which he is worth employing because it is bad to let a person who is capable of work rot away in idleness and become a burden to himself and to others. But both criteria lead to the same conclusion.

Capitalist society does not, and cannot, work in this way. Private employers cannot be expected, save in a few individual cases here and there, to employ workers unless they can see a prospect of profit as a result of employing them. If they did, they would soon go bankrupt. This difference between the social and the capitalist point of view arises from perfectly definite causes. Society, unless it is prepared to let people die of starvation, has to maintain all its members out of the total product of its labours: there is no one else on whom the burden can be thrust. The private employer, when he sacks a man, is free of all further responsibility for him. He can and does thrust off the burden of paying the man on someone else—either on some other employer, if the man can find another job, or on society as a whole. Therefore, under capitalism, men go unemployed even when it would pay to employ them *from the social point of view.*

This is a root defect of capitalist industry; and it becomes, as we have seen, an increasingly serious defect as capitalism comes to be more and more dominated by monopoly. For, as any economist will tell you, the monopolist usually stops employing men at an earlier point than the competitive capitalist. The older economists used even sometimes to deny that 'involuntary unemployment' could exist at all, because, they said, everyone could find some competitive capitalist willing to employ him if he would only accept a low enough wage. I do not think this was ever true; but it was once less obviously untrue than it is nowadays. The monopolist does not go on employing men as long as he can make *any* profit by employing them, as the competitive employer is largely driven to do. The monopolist stops short at the point at which his total profit is largest in relation to the capital he is using; and this means that he stops when he is afraid that more production will mean that he will have to reduce his price, and thus spoil the market. Monopolists, in nine cases out of ten, prefer scarcity to plenty because scarcity means high prices. But scarcity of goods means scarcity of employment as well.

The purpose of Socialist planning is to set the whole people to work making useful things or rendering useful services for the general benefit. The purpose of the measures outlined in the preceding chapter is to make this possible, and therewith to reduce the number of people who are unable to make provision out of their own earnings for the maintenance of themselves and their dependants. But, even when we have done all we can do, in the near future, to bring this about, the problem of poverty will not have been solved, though its dimensions will have been very greatly reduced. Wages, as we have seen, take no account of the number of persons who have to be maintained out of them, or of those persons' needs. A man who has ten children gets no more, for that reason, than a bachelor: a man who has an ailing wife and a sick child needing expensive care gets no more than a man whose family is strong and able to look after itself. A man who is partly disabled through an accident becomes a 'compensation case', and gets a lower income than before; for earnings are related to what a man can produce. If, as a result of his accident, his needs increase, the wage-system takes no account of that.

Accordingly, even if we so rearrange our affairs that everyone who is willing and able to work can always find a job, poverty will remain. It will continue to afflict large families, families which have special needs, and families whose principal breadwinner is disabled. It will also, unless we radically amend our methods of providing for the sick, continue to afflict a great number of households at times when the principal breadwinner is ill and temporarily unable to work. It will afflict many of the aged, unless we become much more generous with old age pensions. It will afflict widows, orphans, and a great number of persons who cannot work owing to physical or mental defects. And the worst thing of all is that it will afflict a great many children who are brought up in such households. Naturally, a high proportion of the nation's children belong to large families; and it is upon such families that the burden of poverty falls most extensively. This factor is aggravated because, on the whole, the worse-paid people have more children than the better paid, as they practise birth-control less. There will remain a formidable problem of poverty even if we adopt the plainly sensible course of ensuring that there shall be work for every able pair of hands.

It ought to be so obvious as hardly to need stating that it is an obligation falling upon any decent human society to give all its members a fair chance in life, to protect all its members from needless suffering, and to deal kindly and helpfully with those who suffer by their own fault. Socialists recognise these obligations, and so do many persons who do not call themselves Socialists. But recognition of this forms no part of our common social tradition, and encounters strong resistances when any attempt is made to base on it the conduct of our public affairs. There are several reasons for this. One set of people is always urged on by the fear that action may be taken which will interfere with 'parental responsibility' and the sacredness of the family as a social unit, and on this ground opposes any suggestion that the State shall assume fresh responsibilities for the children of the nation. At one time, these upholders of 'family life' used to oppose State-provided education, or medical inspection or treatment, or in effect any of the public services which we have now come to accept as normal and necessary. They no longer oppose these services; but they do still oppose any extension of them, however strong the case for it may be.

A second body of opinion, overlapping but by no means identical with the first, is against State action on the ground that it undermines 'individual responsibility', and makes men look to the State for help instead of helping themselves. This form of opposition comes into play mainly when it is suggested that anything should be done to help grown-up men and women. Like the advocates of 'family responsibility', its advocates usually accept what has been done, after opposing it up to the last moment, and thereafter oppose the doing of anything more. Their attitude is illustrated very well by the long struggle over factory legislation, which began early in the nineteenth century and is still going on to-day. The opponents of the Factory Acts began by opposing, on grounds of complete *laissez-faire*, the legal regulation of child labour, even when it was admitted that children of five years and upwards were being commonly employed for as many as twelve and fourteen hours a day. Driven to concede this point, they then opposed the regulation of the labour of young persons and women, until the repeated exposures of ghastly abuses in the factories compelled them to cede that point. Thereafter, they continued to fight tooth and nail against any regulation applying to adult men. Sequences of terrible colliery accidents forced the hand of Parliament, and compelled it to agree to special regulations in the case of coal miners—a principle thereafter extended to certain other dangerous trades. But even to this day the regulations in the Factory Acts about hours of labour do not apply directly to men, though of course many men who work in the same factories as women and young persons actually get the benefit of them. Similarly, wage-regulations have, with a very few exceptions, been applied only to trades in which women predominate. We still act in general on the assumption that adult men ought to be capable of looking after themselves, despite the accumulation of a vast body of evidence which shows that a great many of them are not. Hence the persistence of abominable wages and conditions in many of the more scattered and unorganised occupations. It is doubtless true that much of the underpaid labour is of inferior mental or physical quality. But surely that is all the more reason for society to accept some responsibility for looking after it. Physical and mental weaklings do not thrive when they are left to stand alone. They deteriorate, and thus make the problem worse.

I have no space to pursue this point here. Anyone who wants fuller evidence can find it in my booklet, *Living Wages*, or in any of the great social surveys of recent years. That the facts, again and again discovered and presented, are persistently ignored, even by many professed reformers (and by most of the Trade Unions), is a clear sign of the continued strength of the tradition that the individual is responsible for his own misfortunes, and that it is none of the State's business to help, unless a special case can be made out on the ground that he is a child, or blind or mentally deficient—or a woman.

A third form of opposition comes from those who, without taking their stand on doctrines of individual or family responsibility, oppose State action on the ground that it will be fatal to the profit-making system. This line of argument has been familiar ever since the economist Nassau Senior coined his much-ridiculed argument that all the capitalists' profits came out of the 'last hour' of employment, so that if even one hour were to be cut off the working day, profits would vanish and industry be brought to a stand. Since that was said, hours of labour have been reduced again and again, usually by Trade Union action, without causing this anticipated disaster. Nevertheless the argument, in a less obviously absurd form, continues to do service. It is argued nowadays that we cannot afford as a society to expand the social services because the costs of expansion will make British industries unable to compete in world markets, or will dry up the supply of capital for investment, or will make it not worth while for the capitalists to go on employing labour.

These arguments are a mixture of falsehood and half-truth. No one denies that the standard of living which a country can afford to its people is limited by their productive power. So much is plain commonsense. No one denies that, if the costs of production in one country are increased above the costs of its competitors, it will lose trade in the goods in which such increases occur: so that limits are set, under international capitalist competition, to the wages and conditions which any trade producing for the world market can afford to pay. Again, no one denies that under capitalism investments are made both for profit and largely out of profits: so that as profits fall there is a double tendency for investment from private sources to decline. But this by no means proves what the opponents of further development of the social services are attempting to prove. For, in the first place, better wages and conditions often lead to higher and better output. Secondly, better wages lead to a larger and more assured home market, less subject than the rest of the market to ups and downs, and therefore tending to steady employment in many trades at a high level. Thirdly, capitalists will be deterred from investing only if they can find more profitable outlets for their money elsewhere—or, in other words, if they are allowed to roam the world looking for profitable lines of development or speculative opportunities regardless of the requirements of their own countries. Fourthly, if capitalists have less money to invest because the State takes it from them to pay out to poorer people, the money does not disappear. The poorer people have it instead, and it is likely to fructify much better in creating a steady demand from them than if it is left to the caprices of the rich. If, as a result of this, too little is invested by private persons, the State can make up the deficiency, by investing itself, on behalf of the community, in the forms of enterprise of which the community stands in most urgent need.

Ah! but here, say the opponents of better social services, is the cloven hoof. You are proposing to use the development of these services as a means of drying up the springs of private enterprise, and then to resort to Socialism as a means of setting again a-flowing the rivers which your own action has dried up. Well, why not? If, as these critics contend, capitalism cannot afford to give each member of the community a fair chance in life and a satisfactory measure of security against its mischances, why not invoke a system which can afford these things, at least to the extent which is necessary for ensuring that they are done? If capitalism cannot provide social security, that is the best argument I know of against allowing the capitalist system to continue. It is indeed precisely because capitalism is failing in this that the need for Socialism is becoming urgent.

But, say the critics, the State has already gone a long way towards providing the social security which you demand. It grants free elementary education to all, and free secondary education to a growing minority. It provides medical and dental inspection free to school children, and subsidises treatment where the need is proved. It allows increasing quantities of free or cheap milk and gives local authorities power to provide free or cheap school meals. It holds the worker insured against both sickness and unemployment, and, when he runs out of benefit in these services, finds other means of relieving his necessities through the Assistance Board or the Public Assistance Committee. It provides, in conjunction with voluntary enterprise, free or cheap hospital services. It grants pensions to the aged, and to some widows. It compels employers to pay compensation to those who are disabled in their service, even when the disablement is not the employer's fault. It pays allowances to the children of the unemployed; and for those who are not covered by special provisions there is always the P.A.C. as a last resort. What more can the poor demand? What more can be given them, without danger of rewarding vice above virtue, and making those who do provide for themselves feel that their less deserving neighbours are being unfairly pampered by the State?

Granted, the State does, in these matters, very much more than it used to do; and the result has been to reduce considerably the lump of human misery. But these social services have developed in a curiously haphazard way, and there are in them still many gaps—to say nothing of the major fault that they are still largely directed to patching up evils which ought not to be allowed to arise. Why, for example, is a workman insured against sickness, whereas his wife and children are not insured? Why are there dependants' allowances for the unemployed, but not for the sick? Why is sickness benefit much lower than unemployment benefit, and why are both, for most households, much below a decent living income? Why does the workman have to contribute, by deductions from his wages, towards the cost of some services and not of others? Why does he have to contribute a much higher proportion of the cost of health insurance than of insurance against unemployment? Why is there a Means Test in some cases and not in others? Why are there so many different Means Tests, with no apparent rhyme or reason? Why do wage-earners get certain services, whereas independent workers, such as small shopkeepers, who are no better off, do not? Why do some services vary from place to place, or in the case of health insurance, from one 'approved society' to another, whereas other services are on a uniform national basis? Why are compensation payments limited to a proportion of previous earnings, irrespective of need? Why are school meals, and school milk, provided in some places and not in others, or provided on quite different conditions? Why cannot the State make up its mind how much it costs to keep a child, instead of adopting a different scale for each service which provides dependants' allowances?

This list of questions could be protracted almost indefinitely. These curious anomalies exist because no one has ever planned the social services as a whole, or set out to provide an all-round system of social security. Particular services have been devised and expanded almost at random, and often rather as electoral assets than for any valid reason of priority of need. Thus, sickness benefit is probably kept low mainly because the politicians do not want to antagonise the great insurance companies and friendly societies—and for the same reason a monstrously wasteful and iniquitous private system of life insurance is allowed to remain in being. Local differences persist largely because rural workers are badly underpaid, and the State is afraid of granting decent social services in the rural areas lest the farm worker should be better off when he is sick or out of work than when he is well and in employment. Similar considerations keep down unemployment insurance to a low income level for fear of exceeding the wages paid in the unorganised trades; and the Assistance Board deliberately operates a 'wages stop' designed, where possible, to prevent public payments from exceeding normal earnings.

The whole thing is a ghastly confusion, and must be so as long as the State refuses to accept any general responsibility for seeing to it that decent wages are paid to those who are in work. For it is a bad thing that men should be paid more for the support of their households when they are out of work than they receive for this purpose when they are in work. But it is a much worse thing that men who are in work should receive so little that this is bound to happen, even when the scales of unemployment benefit and assistance are so low as to provide barely enough, or even not enough, for the maintenance of mere physical health, without any allowance for any of the amenities of life.

There is no possible way of escape from this dilemma except by dealing with the incomes of those who are in employment. There are two possible methods of doing this; or, of course, the two can be combined. One method is to extend the legal regulation of wages, which now applies to only a few—mainly women's—trades, to all trades, partly by establishing new

Trade Boards with power to fix legal minimum rates, and partly by laying down absolute minima, at less than which it would be unlawful for anyone to be employed. The other method is that of bringing up the effective incomes of those who have plainly too little by means of subsidies from the State, either in money or in kind.

Personally, I favour a combination of these methods. In my booklet, *Living Wages*, I have tried to show that many of the occupations in which the lowest wages are paid are not in depressed industries, and that these low wages exist, not because the industries cannot afford to pay more, but because labour is to be had at so low a price. There are in all our cities as well as in the countryside large numbers of workers who are almost wholly devoid of bargaining power. One reason why they are not organised in Trade Unions, and why Trade Unions do nothing for them, is that they are too poor to afford Trade Union contributions. They are forced to take whatever jobs they can get, at whatever wages they are offered. A few years ago the Unemployment Insurance Statutory Committee compiled for its own purposes a list of the trades in which it had found grown-up men earning less than 25s. a week. This list included the following: dance-hall attendant, cinema commissionaire, barman, greyhound-racing kennelman, cinema operator, garage hand, fishmonger's assistant, as well as a number of others which can by no stretch of imagination be regarded as belonging to the category of depressed trades. These wages are paid simply because our civilisation leaves everywhere a scum of derelict humanity, never apprenticed to any regular occupation, and drifting about from one ill-paid job to another without hope of betterment.

Such conditions are a scandal; and there is no way of remedying them except by legal regulation of wages. If it is argued that the men in question cannot have been worth any more, the Report of the same Committee supplies the answer. Out of 389 adult men who were getting less than 25s. a week (in 1937) the Committee found only 22 to be suffering from any definite physical disability, 24 to be of specially low mental quality, and 11 to be advanced in age—leaving 332 who were being disgracefully sweated for reasons other than these. Moreover, in most cases the employers' only answer, when they were asked why such incredibly low wages were being paid, was that the *occupations*—not the man, mark you!—were 'of an inferior type'. Probably most of the men were in fact also 'of an inferior type'. Who would not be, after existing for long at such a standard as these wages imply?

Of course, some of the very low wages were in depressed trades—in the cotton industry, for example—but most were not. There are some trades which would practically disappear if they were compelled to pay a living wage to all their workers; and there are others in which fewer persons would be employed, as a result either of smaller production or of increased use of machinery. Is it desirable to keep industries alive on these terms? And is it not very much better to substitute machinery where manual labour is retained only because it can be paid a sweated wage?

I admit, however, that in practice there are so many trades in which sweated wages are still being paid that it would be difficult to raise all wages to a tolerable standard at all quickly without causing a good deal of dislocation. I want the abnormally low raised as far and as fast as possible; and I am sure a General Minimum Wage Act, including an extension of the Trade Board system, is the best way of bringing this about. It is, however, impracticable rapidly to raise wages to a level which will provide a decent living income for the larger families; and accordingly it is necessary to resort in addition to increasing the bottom incomes by other means.

The way of doing this which I have always favoured is by the grant of family allowances—that is, of a supplementary income, payable to the mother, for each child under school age or attending school. I want this allowance to be paid by the State, out of money raised by general taxation; for this is the only fair way. It will not do to call on the individual private employer to pay it—for that would cause him to discriminate against employing married men. An 'employers' pool' is objectionable, because the allowance ought to be paid whether a man is an employed person or not, and whether or not he is for the moment in work. It ought not to be cancelled when a worker is stood off, or sick, or on strike, or out of a job; for his wife and children, as well as he, need food and clothing none the less under such conditions. Payment by means of an employers' pool would put too much power into the employers' hands, and would fail to recognise that the payment represents a claim on society as a whole, rather than on any particular industry or on industry in general. Finally, any proposal to put the allowances on a contributory basis would be objectionable, because the workers are already paying too much by way of deductions from wages, and, even if they could afford more, it ought to go to improving the existing contributory services and not to paying for new ones.

The State, then, ought to pay, raising the required sum by means of general taxation. But at this point in come the critics from two sides, to object that this plan also is contrary to the best interests of the workers themselves. Trade Union leaders—not all, but some of them—argue that family allowances would be used for the purpose of reducing wages, or at all events for preventing wage advances, and would thus hurt the main body of wage-earners more than they would help the 'bottom dogs'. I do not deny that, *in time of war*, when the State really controls wages, family allowances might be adduced as a reason for not raising wages to keep pace with the cost of living. I do entirely deny that, *in time of peace*, they could possibly weaken the bargaining power of the Trade Unions. On the contrary, they would be bound to strengthen it, by giving the workers more power to stand out against taking an unduly low wage. And, in war-time, to the extent to which there really is not enough to allow the previous standard of living to be kept up, have not the larger families the prior claim to what can be spared?

The Trade Union case against family allowances, as it affects peace-time conditions, rests on a sheer misunderstanding. As it affects war conditions, it has some validity as long as incomes other than wages are left uncontrolled—but only because one injustice leads to another.

The other line of criticism is more plausible. The State, it is argued, can in practice afford only a limited sum for all the social services taken together. To the extent to which it is desired to relieve large families, is it not better to do this by grants in kind—school milk, school meals, more scholarships with maintenance allowances, better health services, and so on—than to dole out money to parents who may fritter it away on drink or gambling, instead of using it for the purposes for which it is given? Well, I want all these other things; and, if I had to choose, I might give any one of them priority over family allowances in cash. But I do not see why I should have to choose: I want both. If the funds are really short, let us have a system of family allowances beginning only when there are two dependent children in the household—which would be relatively cheap. But let us have at least this; for no system of relief in kind that I have seen really provides for all the disabilities under which the large, poor household labours, or is capable of giving the children in such households a reasonable chance of a fair start in life.

Let us begin, then, by demanding that, in one way or another, every household in our community shall normally receive a tolerable living income, large enough at any rate to bring its members above Mr. Rowntree's poverty line. It is a matter of the second order of importance how much of this income is to be paid in return for work done, and how much on the score of need to those who are not able to earn enough, or how much is to be paid in cash, and how much in kind through the extension of communal services. The important thing is to banish sheer want altogether; and the first necessary steps towards this are those which have just been outlined.

It is necessary to do more than raise wages and supplement them by allowances in the case of the larger families. A man who is sick, or has sickness in his home, needs more and not less income than when he and his family are in health. There is no excuse for not bringing sickness benefit up to a tolerable living standard—at least up to Mr. Rowntree's 'human needs' minimum, or for continuing to exclude wives, children and the non-wage-earning population from the use of the public medical services. There ought to be a thoroughly adequate general practitioner service, with specialist services to supplement it, open to everybody who cares to use it; and this State Medical Service ought to be linked up with a fully equipped hospital service for all types of accident or disease. The voluntary hospitals and the hospitals owned by local authorities ought to be fused and expanded to form this new hospital service; and with it there ought to be developed a proper system of convalescent homes, clinics, and all the incidentals of an adequate all-round medical service. I feel sure, too, that the whole of the service should be free; for it is the right course for the State to encourage people to seek medical advice and treatment in good time, instead of waiting until disease has established a firm hold over them.

If a man needs his income when he is ill, he needs it also when he is unemployed. The aim of the State, as we have seen, should be, first of all, to prevent unemployment; and the need to relieve it on any large scale is in itself a confession of failure. But some unemployment will remain, even if the State sets out deliberately to prevent it; and no man or woman who is unemployed ought to get less than the Rowntree minimum income. It is not, however, enough merely to relieve the unemployed. The utmost endeavour should be made to train them for useful work. A worker may have lost his job because his trade has declined. If so, he should be trained for another. He may have lost it because he has been out of health. If so, plans should be made for restoring his vigour. He may have lost it through his own fault. If so, he should be given the chance of amendment in accordance with the nature of his failing. Above all, no boy or girl should ever be allowed to grow up without being trained both for a definite trade and in a general 'handiness' which will make them able to pick up another easily should need arise. It is a grave fault of our present educational system that it does not provide for this: many of the 'unemployables' and failures of later years are products of an educational system which remains entirely uncertain of the purposes for which the education is given.

On that point I shall have more to say later. For the present, my concern is with the unemployed. When this war ends there will be a vast demobilisation of men and women from the armed forces, the auxiliary services, the munition factories, and all the establishments in which they will have been temporarily taking someone else's place. There is an immense danger, unless these workers are given a proper chance, of reproducing on a vaster scale what happened at the end of the last war, when thousands upon thousands of young men came out of the Army without having ever learnt a trade, and were simply left to fend for themselves in a world where jobs were scarce. There will be, this time, the advantage that as war becomes more highly mechanised the armed services themselves have to give a larger proportion of their recruits some training which can be made useful in civilian life. But both for them and for the discharged munition workers the acquired aptitudes of war-time will need careful redirection in order to fit them in with the needs of peace. There will have to be re-training on an immense scale for the requirements of post-war industry; and if this task is ignored or scamped there will be a disastrous manufacture of 'unemployables' and misfits, and a consequent lowering of the country's productive capacity and ability to yield to all its citizens a decent standard of life.

Men and women, while they are undergoing this re-training, will have to be maintained at proper civilian standards; for if anyone thinks the unwanted soldiers will consent to remain in the armed forces and be re-trained away from their wives and families under any conditions he is very wide of the mark. In these cases, too, the Rowntree minimum will have to apply—adjusted, of course, according to the level of prices as it exists in the after-war period.

A decent minimum standard of living for the employed, the sick, the unemployed, and those who are training for employment—how far does that carry us towards the 'social security' at which we ought to aim? A longish way, but by no means all the way. For there remain the wholly or partly disabled, the chronically infirm, the aged—in fact all who are regularly unable to earn a decent living; and there remain also the groups of war-ruined persons who are not able to find openings in the post-war world, and are not suitable for ordinary wage-earning or training for a new trade. In effect, there remains the whole problem of pensions—in the wide sense of providing incomes for those adults who, for one reason or another, are unable to maintain themselves.

Reformers, impressed by the prevalence of unemployment, have generally wanted to provide retiring pensions at the lowest age possible, in order to relieve congestion in the labour market. But, if the State does its business properly, there will be no such congestion in the future. Especially, in that event, the country will need, during the years immediately after the war, all the hands it can get to help with the repair of war damage, the making up of arrears of ordinary work, and the building of a new Britain better adapted to furnish a good life for all its citizens. Under these circumstances an early retiring age will be undesirable, except for those who suffer from actual infirmity. It will be requisite, rather, to keep as many people as possible at work, supplementing their wages where they are no longer able to earn enough to meet their human needs. Pensions will be needed, not for the old as such, but for those of any age who are prevented by any cause from doing useful work. Such non-State services as workmen's compensation will have to be taken over; and there will have to be a general arrangement for pensioning off the unfit, old or young, and for granting supplementary incomes to those who are still able to do light or part-time work. Moreover, all these pensions and allowances will have to be on a scale which assures at least the Rowntree minimum standard to every recipient.

Clearly, these conditions of social security ought not to

apply to wage-earners only. Anyone who needs them ought to be eligible. The small shopkeeper who loses his business, or is no longer equal to carrying it on; the farmer who is past his work, and is not getting the best out of the land; the superseded of all occupations and callings ought to be able to come to the State, not merely for an old age pension at an age arbitrarily fixed, but whenever the need for succour comes upon them. The State could then say to them: 'You do not really need a pension: you need help, while we train you for another job'; or it could say: 'Yes, you are past work: we will see to it that you pass the rest of your days in reasonable security.'

No doubt this implies a 'Means Test' and a 'Fitness Test' too. Why not? Nobody has a right to be maintained at the public expense without working for his keep, if his work is worth having. Nor has anyone a right to be maintained if he is in a perfectly good position to maintain himself. This second condition involves awkward problems about the extent to which anyone who applies for public help ought to be compelled to sell his possessions and live on the proceeds. The old Poor Law used to work on the principle that only the sheerly 'destitute' had any claim to relief. We say nowadays that it is a crime to compel a man to sell his house, or dissipate his small savings, before the State will consent to relieve his distress. But there must be lines drawn somewhere. A man cannot reasonably ask for relief in order to enable him to keep up a large mansion: nor can he reasonably refuse to apply the income from his savings towards his maintenance, provided some minimum sum is disregarded in calculating his needs as a recognition that he has done what he could to help himself.

These considerations suggest that we shall need after the war, as an instrument for stopping the gaps in our system of social security, something arising out of the existing Assistance Board, but with much wider powers and a quite different basic principle of action. For the criterion in the new era will have to be, not 'How little can we give this household without letting it fall into positive destitution and physical distress?' but 'How much does this household need to ensure a tolerable satisfaction of human needs, spiritual as well as merely physical?' and 'What can we do, in order to put the members of this household in the best possible way for serving the community usefully in the future?'

There remains one matter, of primary importance in this connection, which has so far in this chapter been passed over almost in silence. That matter is education, which is destined to undergo a remarkable revolution as soon as we decide to act on the principle that it is the State's business to make the best of the nation's productive capacity, and to see that every citizen is made use of according to his abilities in the common service. Merely by assuring to every household a decent basic standard of living we shall save an enormous waste of potential ability and productive power that is allowed to go on at present. We shall get away, especially if we provide everywhere proper school meals, proper medical and dental treatment, and proper opportunities for healthy recreation, from most of the stunting of children, in both body and mind, that arises out of malnutrition and evil nurture in the early years of life. We shall not, of course, be able to escape altogether from the consequences of bad heredity or parental incapacity; but we shall be in a position to salve and develop a far larger proportion of the capacity of the nation's children than at present, and to look forward confidently to a steady improvement in the average mental and physical quality of our citizens.

Over and above this, we shall be approaching our educational problems in a quite different spirit from that which has prevailed in the past. Hitherto, access to secondary education has meant for the children of working-class parents mainly an opportunity of rising out of the working class; and all higher education has tended to be given a marked bias against what is called 'vocational training'. In truth, the book education which finds favour in our higher schools is hardly, if at all, less vocational than what is called by that appellation. It consists largely of training boys and girls to become teachers and clerks rather than artisans or housewives. There is some excuse for this in the need for teachers and in the multiplication of clerical jobs which is the outcome of capitalism at its present 'financial' stage. This works out very badly; for it leads to the development of secondary and other higher schools, not as an open and practical preparation for the vocations most of these pupils intend to follow, but rather as bastard imitators of the culture provided in our older 'public' schools for the education of a limited governing class. It leads to the most intensive cultivation of the 'old school tie' among those whose old school tie is newest; and it tends to breed snobs and would-be 'gentlemen', instead of citizens well equipped for playing their part in the ordinary work of society. The actual education is perverted less in the case of science students than elsewhere, because science is so closely related to the practical affairs of living that education 'in the air' in scientific subjects is nearly out of the question. But the scientists, and even the students in confessedly Technical Colleges, are no less affected than the others by the snobbery and by the sense that a superior education is meant for a superior class, and therefore gives them a claim to social and economic superiority.

Many teachers strive against these tendencies; and of course not all pupils are affected by them. But they are very prevalent, and are encouraged by the very structure of the English educational system. For the State system of education in England began as an attempt to provide schooling on the cheap for the children of the lower classes, quite apart from the more expensive and 'superior' schooling provided for the children of the rich; and this dualism still dominates English education, even when many Grammar Schools have resorted to the local authorities for financial aid and many minor 'public schools' provide much worse education than the better secondary schools established by the local authorities.

Despite this dualism, the quality of primary education has greatly improved in recent years, and most of the secondary schools are of high standard in what they teach. But the entire system is sadly lacking in clarity of social objective, and will remain so as long as the dualism is left in being. What is needed of public education is that it should produce intelligent citizens, equipped to understand the world in which they will have to work and to apply what they have learned at school to the practical problems with which that world presents them. For these purposes, there is no special value in 'cultural' as against 'vocational' subjects: what really matters is the spirit in which a subject is taught. The present system leads to an absurd undervaluation of manual ability, to an absurd lack of encouragement for the artistic and creative impulses, and to the turning out of a high proportion of persons who have been given no real opportunity of understanding the world they will have to live in. The majority of those who go on to some form of secondary education leave school by the time they are sixteen. Instead of being educated with this in view, they often receive half of an education framed for those who are to stay at school until eighteen and are then to go on to a University. On the other hand, those who do remain at school till eighteen are apt to leave it with no knowledge of how to use their hands, except for games, and with only the foggiest notions about the technical basis of modern life; and the scientists, who do get this technical knowledge, at any rate up to a point, are all too apt to know nothing else, and to have no grasp at all of how their country is governed and barely a nodding acquaintance with the great cultural traditions out of which our civilisation has grown.

To reform these abuses is not mainly a matter of changing educational administration, or even of amending the curriculum, necessary as both these things are. The educational system will come straight only to the extent to which society as a whole has clear objectives, and therewith a knowledge of the purposes which education is to serve. All that we can do, at this stage, is to make up our minds to give every child the fullest opportunity of profiting by all the education it wants and is capable of receiving, and to keep our minds wide open to the new, creative ideas that will blossom as fast as we set our conceptions of society in order. As soon as society itself is planned for plenty and for assuring the essentials of the good life to all its citizens, the teachers will know what they are called upon to do, and there will be vast changes in education which it is at present impossible to predict. Book-learning will lose its exclusive prestige; and craftsmanship and artistic creativeness will receive their appropriate recognition. Education will become destandardised in its higher ranges, even while the minimum common standard of attainment in its lower ranges is improved. The technical will cease to be looked down upon, as its social purpose becomes clearer, and it will be differently taught, with greater social meaning and cultural content. The literary will cease to be purely literary, and will be related more closely to the art of living in the world of to-day. There will be growing pains, of course; but teachers will be happier, given a clearer purpose; and I think happy, and not thwarted, teachers are the first essential for a successful educational régime.

What this means in terms of the form and quantity of education I do not profess to know at all clearly. I am sure it is of the first importance that education in some meaningful form shall continue right through adolescence and shall lead right on to adult education in forms much more diverse and appealing to more various temperaments than those of to-day. I am sure that our schools—and especially our higher schools—ought to be much more closely related to the general life of the community than they now are—that they ought, for example, to be linked up with community centres and recreative clubs which would bring people of different ages and occupations together on a basis of neighbourliness. I am sure that it is no better—and no worse—to learn Latin than Chemistry, and that both can be taught either as lifeless memorising or as embodiments of living human values. I care much less what boys and girls learn than how they learn it; and I dislike equally the cultured superiority of the follower of antique disciplines and the practical narrowness of the trainer of mere brain-fodder for the economic machine. It is possible to help boys and girls to grow up good workers, good citizens, and good human beings, with a love for beauty and truth and justice and for doing a job well. But this—the proper end of education—is not possible in a community that knows neither where it is nor whither it is trying to go.

I have sought in this chapter to define in broad terms the requirements of social security and well-being for the ordinary man and woman, as far as these ends can be promoted by collective action. I am led, at the end of my exposition, to this, that the power of the State to make men and women healthy and happy depends on the intensity with which those who control the State themselves seek these ends and believe it possible to attain them. For we never know what we can do until we really try; and most of us never really try until some of us—a sufficient influential number—really believe. The State takes its capacity, as well as its quality, from the faith of its more active and courageous citizens. 'Social security' may seem to some an uncourageous ideal—a desire for shelter rather than adventure. But the attainment of it demands a high adventurousness in those who make its general diffusion their objective; and it has in it the capacity, if we can attain to it, of releasing a vast amount of creative energy that is now stifled in childhood and adolescence, or thwarted in adult life by a sense of futility arising out of the apparent aimlessness of the society in which we live. My case for Socialism is, in this connection, that it does provide a clear and worth-while objective—witness the tremendous social forces which have been released by it during the past twenty years in the Soviet Union, where it has had its chance. I want a similar chance here, in order not that we may imitate the Russians, but that we may strike out in our own way towards an equalitarian society that will build upon our own liberal traditions a new scheme of values and, in making fresh conquests for humanity, will not throw away the conquests that our fathers have made.

NOTE.—This chapter was written before the publication of the Beveridge Report, which reinforces many of its conclusions.

V

A WORLD IN TRAVAIL

But what security can we have by seeking merely security for ourselves? None at all. The entire programme of social security means nothing, unless we seek it internationally as well as within our own frontiers, or unless we can make the world safe from a recurrence of the devastation which has already swept over most of Europe and Asia, and is threatening other continents as well. We all know this nowadays, as we have never known it before. Hitler has taught us that lesson, though the last war failed to teach it us; and we are in no danger of forgetting it for the moment. That danger will come later, when the war is over, and the statesmen, of whatever party, sit down to settle the configuration of the new Europe and the new world.

What sort of Europe, and what sort of world, are we looking to them to make, with our aid and that of all the suffering peoples? It is of no profit, in answering this question, to indulge ourselves in dreams. There have been enough fine phrases uttered since 1918 to make most of us tired of hearing them. We want something a great deal solider than phrases about international goodwill, or than the Covenant of the ill-fated League of Nations. We want a solid, matter-of-fact settlement that will truly bring peace and prosperity because it involves real co-operation among the peoples and not more phrase-mongering by the politicians at Geneva or Versailles.

What has the experience of the past decades taught us—what, I mean, that can be helpful to us in facing the problems of to-morrow? Foremost I should put the lesson that unilateral disarmament of the vanquished will not work, at any rate within the framework of State Sovereignty and national independence which the Versailles covenant-makers insisted on preserving intact. If a nation is 'sovereign', among other 'sovereign' nations, nothing will stop it from rearming if its rulers want rearmament. The States which are supposed to be responsible for enforcing disarmament must, if they are to achieve their purpose, police the defeated country with large armed forces, not merely for a brief period but indefinitely—for as long as they police it national resentment will continue, and as soon as they cease to police it rearmament will begin. The burden of this policing will soon become intolerable, if it is attempted, both to the soldiers and to those who have to foot the bill. Before long, one of the policing countries will weary of the job, and withdraw its contingent, and the victors will begin to squabble among themselves.

That is one lesson of the last peace. A second is that it does not pay to impoverish the vanquished. Reparations were not gain but loss to those who attempted to exact them. They upset world trade, provoked world depression, and, even apart from their share in bringing on this war, caused much more economic loss than they were worth. Again, punitive measures against the trade of the vanquished, apart from their evil political effects, impoverish the world; for it is true, as the economists tell us, that nations thrive by one another's prosperity. It is, for example, out of the question for Central and Eastern Europe to prosper if the Germans are too poor to be able to buy their produce. Possibly, if a great country could be simply wiped off the map, as Hitler has repeatedly expressed his intention of wiping off Great Britain, the sore would be healed in time, and a reorientation of world trade could come about. But in the meantime there would be great suffering in the countries which have depended on the British market. Moreover, if a country is not wiped off the map, but only impoverished, the trouble continues as long as the poverty lasts.

A third lesson is that it is impracticable to persuade States which enjoy political independence to co-operate effectively in economic matters under the capitalist system. Each national group of capitalists will inevitably seek to use its State for its own ends, and to push off its difficulties on the other countries. Each group of capitalists in the large States will want its State to pursue imperialist policies at the expense of others, because such policies can be turned to its profit. And, where the capitalists themselves form international combines transcending the frontiers of their States, no State will be able to control their doings, or to prevent them from exploiting the common people.

I realise that this way of putting the case conflates two lessons into one. I am putting the blame at once on national sovereignty and on the capitalist system; whereas they are two quite different things. They are different; but they are also very closely connected. Historically, the independent Sovereign State has developed side by side with capitalism, and as its instrument. Each State has been, for its own capitalists, the protector of the rights of property at home and abroad, the defender of merchants and mercantilist empire-builders and concession-hunters in their foreign adventures, the guardian of its bankers and financiers in the high realms of international exchange, and, in sum, the exponent of the interests of its own capitalists whenever these have clashed with the interests of others. Nor is this either mere accident, or the mere result of deep-laid capitalist plotting. It is unavoidable. If the State allows the property of the nation to be owned and controlled by a body of private profit-seekers, it is bound to protect that property, which is the source of public revenue and of the people's livelihood none the less for being under such control. If the national capitalists lose, the State loses revenue, and the workers lose their jobs. It is a necessary condition of things that where private capitalism and the nation State coexist, they shall work together. Nothing will alter that.

A fourth lesson of the inter-war period is that equality between big States and little States, on a basis of coequal independent sovereignty, is fudge. Little States cannot be really independent, either politically or economically, except on sufferance. In the world of to-day the little State is powerless in arms against its great neighbours, who can at will merely brush it aside or trample it underfoot. No little State can afford, or has the resources, to maintain an army or a navy or an air force capable of resisting the armed forces of a great State even for long enough to make the great State think twice about attacking it, or to give time for other States to come to its assistance, if they will. The armed forces of little States are futile, unless they act as mere auxiliaries of some greater power. Nor can a little State hope to equip its forces except by purchases from great States; for only great States possess the all-round industrial equipment that is needed for modern war.

Nor can the little States be independent economically. They have to link their currencies to those of their greater neighbours, and to adjust their economies to fit in with their greater neighbours' needs. If there seems here and there an exception to this rule—for example, Sweden—it arises owing to good fortune in the possession of exceptionally sought-for materials, and has the disadvantage of making the little State more an object of the covetousness of a predatory Great Power.

In the make-believe of Geneva politics, the little States were able to some extent to play at equality. But their fate and future were none the less settled for them by the behaviour of the few Great Powers.

The fifth lesson we should have learnt by this time is that capitalism, whatever its past achievements may have been, is no longer capable of creating plenty, or of keeping the peoples at work, or of developing the world's resources for the enrichment of the common man. Everywhere the great capitalist has become a clamourer for monopolistic privilege, a declaimer against the evils of 'unregulated output', a destroyer of what he calls 'redundant capacity', a purchaser of new inventions and new sources of material supply, not for the purpose of exploiting them to the full, but lest some rival get hold of them and use them to create unwanted plenty. Each group of capitalists clamours for tariffs, quotas, restrictions on the freedom of trade, and each does its best to limit the right of entry of new competitors into its trade or market. Each big capitalist is active in buying up smaller capitalists, in order to put them out of business; and the smaller capitalists, too, organise, wherever they can, restrictive trade associations to control the conditions of sale and prevent the bane of cheapness. The apologists of capitalism are no longer able to declaim proudly that capitalism means 'freedom of enterprise': they have to talk stuff about the virtues of 'rationalisation' instead. But 'rationalisation' usually means shutting down somebody else's factory in order to increase your power of exploiting the consumers.

These are the five lessons which every open-minded person ought to have learnt by now. May I be allowed briefly to repeat them?

1. It is impossible, within a system of independent, sovereign States, effectively to hold a great State disarmed for long.

2. It does not pay a people (though it may pay particular capitalists) to impoverish another people; for peoples thrive by one another's prosperity.

3. Under capitalism, effective international co-operation between independent sovereign States is impossible, because each State must seek to serve the interests of its own capitalists, on whom production, employment, and taxable capacity depend as long as they are left in economic control.

4. Big States and little States cannot, in the world of to-day, live side by side on terms of real equality, either political or economic.

5. Capitalism has shown plainly its incapacity to make the best use of the resources of production, and has become more and more given over to monopoly, restrictiveness and the extermination of the smaller fry by the great Leviathans.

If these are the lessons, what morals are we to draw from them for our practical guidance? The plain and conclusive commonsense of the matter is that it will not serve our purpose to put back the old Europe which Hitler has destroyed. If we were able to do that, as the sequel to military victory, we should merely be letting ourselves in for another generation of artificial poverty and, before it was over, for another world war. Even this would be better for the spirit of man than a victory of Nazi savagery; but it is not what any sensible person will set out to accomplish, unless he is blinded by nationalism, or wicked enough to put capitalist self-interest before public welfare. Petty politicians and timid monarchs may seek such ends, because they cannot face the idea of a Europe in which they can no longer strut about as dignitaries. Purblind nationalists may seek such ends, because they cannot see that the real spirit of the nation can best find scope to express itself within a planned, supranational order. Fools may seek such ends, because they demand no thinking, and require only loyalty to a dead tradition. Capitalist knaves may seek such ends, because they can see that it will be easier to wangle petty politicians than the leaders of a new world order. Ordinary sensible people, who want to make the world richer and more secure, and to be given a rest from fighting and a chance to live lives of their own, will seek ends essentially different. They will want a world order strong enough to prevent war and to supersede monopoly, to plan for plenty instead of scarcity, and to make their ends, rather than the ends of politicians or kings or financiers or monopolists, the ends aimed at by government, and guaranteed by the fundamental character of the social system.

If we are to plan for a supranational order, *how* are we to plan for it? And, if we are to plan for a system which will get away from capitalist restrictionism and release the powers of plenty upon the peoples, how are we to reconcile planning for such a system with the immediate need to mobilise every possible ally against the Nazis' attempt to dominate the world? Plainly, among the forces which we must use for the defeat of the Nazis is nationalism; and nationalism seems at present to stand for a negation of the supranational order which alone can guarantee peace and security. Our difficult task is to convince the nationalists that the true interest of nationalism lies, not in sovereign independence, but in collaboration in the task of building up a supranational order, and at the same time to convince the peoples that they will never get security by 'minding their own business', but only by minding the world's business, with which their own is inextricably mingled up. If we want peace in Europe, or between Europe and other continents, we must have, as a foundation for it, a social order which can ensure peace and prosper by its continuance. Short of this, we are offered nothing except a perpetuation of international rivalries, and, as their outcome, nothing except a Nazi-dominated Europe, armed to the teeth for war, and recking nothing of the people's welfare save to the extent to which 'illfare' is bound to affect adversely the projects of the superior race—the system, in effect, of the slave plantation, where the master cares for his servants' welfare precisely to the extent to which 'welfare' is a means to his own profit.

The true values of nationality are cultural values. They do not require the possession of absolute political sovereignty or of economic self-determination regardless of wider common interests. They do require self-government in those matters which affect the individual in his daily, significant relations with other men. They require the use of the national language in public as well as private affairs, the education of children in a knowledge of the national culture and traditions, the freedom to celebrate the national anniversaries and to cultivate the national genius in the arts and amenities of life, and the local self-government of the people in all those matters which can be effectively managed within the boundaries of the nation. They require that the officials who look after the nation's affairs shall speak the national language and participate in the national habits of thought, and that the transgressor shall be punished by men of his own kind and judged by his peers who share with him the traditions of the nation. But these requirements of nationality are fully consistent with obligations to a larger social unit, and with the organisation of major economic and political affairs over an area wider than that of the nation. This must be so if nationality is to survive; for national isolationism is evidently inconsistent with the technical conditions of the modern world. Nations, in the twentieth century, cannot live to themselves alone: they must either devise ways of managing their affairs in common or submit to having them managed for them by a 'superior' nation which has converted nationalism into imperialism and assigned to itself the mission of lording it over other nations as the chosen people of history.

There is nothing which ordinary men and women want which they cannot enjoy as free partners within a supranational order. They can have, within such an order, the governance of national and local affairs in their own language and by national officials of their own choosing. They can have freedom of association, freedom to develop their national predilections and cultural practices, freedom to celebrate their national festivals and achievements, freedom to worship God, or not to worship Him, in their own ways. But nationalists have to recognise that most nations are too small to be fully independent in a world which has gone as far as this world of ours in conquering the forces of nature. The independent nation is as obsolete to-day as the independent city became with the rise of the Nation-State some centuries ago. The nation cannot live, nowadays, to itself alone. It must either dominate other nations—and only large nations can aspire to domination—or be dominated itself, or seek escape from this dilemma in the creation of a supranational comity of nations in which there is neither domination nor being dominated. An island nation, such as Eire, or a mountain nation, such as Switzerland, may try to hide itself away from the knowledge of this truth. But unless the other nations of Europe succeed in establishing for themselves a supranational form of government, such nations as these cannot stand. They will be swept away, and absorbed into the empires of greater nations, unless the peoples of Europe unite over an area which transcends the nation.

If this unity is to be real, it must be built upon sure economic foundations. The peoples of Europe must set to work to develop their common estate, which consists of all the natural riches of the continent, all the capital resources that have been created by the labour of men upon these riches, and all the man-power and intelligence that are at hand for labouring upon them to-day. There must be, for the direction of this labour, a common economic plan; and for the proper execution of this plan there must be a structure of common services, co-ordinated over the entire supranational territory. There must be, for example, a unified transport system, based on international control of the main railways, waterways and road systems and on an international mercantile marine and an international air service. There must be a co-ordinated power system, based on a general plan of electrical development, which will use the resources of coal and oil and water power to carry a supply of cheap electric current to every part of the continent. There must be an international system of communications, including an internationally controlled radio service both for the dissemination of news and for the stimulation of international consciousness among the peoples.

Nor is it less important that the basic industries of mining, metal manufacture, and the production of machinery and aircraft shall pass under international control, both because these are the industries on which depends the production of armaments, and because they are pre-eminently the suppliers of capital goods. Concerted planning for Europe means that the work of industrial development will have to be planned for the entire continent, and that it will be a matter for international decision what types of investment in new productive equipment are to be made, and where they are to be located. This is a vital matter; for one of the most formidable tasks of the new Europe will be to forward the industrialisation of the more backward areas. Without further industrialisation, such countries as Poland and Jugoslavia are bound to languish in poverty and to be oppressed by over-population. The development of their resources, so far from affecting adversely the industries of the already developed areas, will provide better markets for them by raising the standards of life. It is neither possible for these countries to provide the capital for their own industrial development without help from outside, nor desirable that this help should take the form of 'foreign investment' by the nationals or the Governments of entirely independent States. Such foreign investment breeds imperialism and the exploitation of one people by another. What is needed is to take the whole business of investment out of the purely national sphere, as far as major economic developments are concerned, and to organise it internationally, as a function of the authority responsible for international planning.

Take, again, the question of 'foreign trade'. Within a unified Europe there ought clearly to be no question of tariffs when goods pass from one country to another. Frontiers within the supranational area ought to be as irrelevant as the 'frontier' between Lancashire and Yorkshire, or between Pennsylvania and New York. Perhaps this sweeping away of tariff barriers is too difficult a thing to be accomplished at a single blow. If so, it will have to be done by stages. But perhaps there is no way, except that of a sudden and complete reversal, of getting it done at all.

It is a different question whether tariffs, or other barriers to trade, should exist at the frontiers of the combined supranational area. To this there is not the same objection—that tariff barriers are inconsistent with the development of a common supranational plan. To plan the production of the entire world under a single authority would be, for the present, too ambitious a venture. Between the great economic units which will dominate world production in the new era there will have to be regulations governing the movement of goods. Tariffs are not, I am sure, the best method of accomplishing this regulation; but I prefer to leave that question aside now and come back to it later on.

If the whole supranational area is to constitute a vast, free internal market, it will evidently need to possess a common currency. Money will have to pass everywhere within it according to a common scheme of values. Central banking will therefore have to be internationalised. There are, moreover, very strong reasons for making the entire banking system international. Any concerted economic plan must be not only a plan of production but also consequently a plan of finance.

The credits required for financing all the various parts of the plan must be forthcoming, and the credit system as a whole must be adjusted to the requirements of supranational planning. One country will no longer be free to attempt to transfer its difficulties to others by monetary manipulation; and the financial policies required for stabilising the flow of production will become matters of supranational concern. All banks, therefore, or rather all banks which either regulate currency and credit conditions or supply credit to producers or traders, will have to become part of the great supranational banking system.

The object of all this planning will be to increase the output of useful goods and services as a means of raising the standard of life. Evidently the purpose in view must be to achieve, as much as possible, an approximation of living standards throughout Europe. There must be a common determination to put an end to the bitter poverty which afflicts many of the peasant countries, and to bring their standards up a great deal nearer to those of the more advanced countries. Economic unification will not of itself bring this about—witness the example of the United States, where the wealth of New York or California exists side by side with primary poverty in the South and in many of the farming areas. Such poverty can be cured only by deliberate action—by capital investment in the backward areas, by intensive education in the arts of production, and by freedom of movement for populations crowded too thickly in territories unsuited for high economic development.

I have tried in the foregoing paragraphs to outline the essential conditions for the development of an effective international economic plan. In doing this I have said nothing of the economic system through which this plan is to be carried out. But it is surely plain enough that no such plan is practicable, and that nothing even remotely resembling it is practicable, except on a basis of common ownership of the essential industries and services. How far would the Soviet Union have advanced with planning over its vast area if the basic resources and instruments of production had been left in private ownership? It is not necessary for planning, either nationally or internationally, that *all* industries and services shall pass into collective ownership. But it is indispensable that the *basic* industries and services, on which the rest depend, shall be directly under the control of those who direct the plan, and shall be carried on, not for the profit of any private person, but for the good of the entire community. When the community itself is international, this implies, for these basic services, not national but international control. The banks, the main means of transport, the power stations, the coal mines, the oil wells, the postal services, and the heavy industries supplying the main materials for the making of capital goods (or armaments)—all these ought to be owned and controlled, not by the separate countries which have entered into a supranational union, but by that union itself.

Thus, the necessary conditions of a planned supranational order lead on directly to Socialism, and to Socialism on a supranational basis. It would be no less disastrous for a single country than for a group of private capitalists to claim the right to misuse its economic resources contrary to the general welfare of the supranational community.

I have a feeling that much of what I have written in this chapter may seem Utopian, or even undesirable, to many of my fellow-Socialists. For though Socialism has always claimed to be an international movement, it has in practice developed mainly on national lines, each national Socialist Party trying to win power in its own country and demanding the national ownership of the essential industries and services by its own State in the interests of its own people. This is natural enough, as long as Socialists, in common with other people, have to work within a framework of independent national sovereign States. They cannot demand that the banks or the coal mines shall be internationally owned when no international body capable of owning or administering them exists. They can work only within the framework of their own States, as long as this framework remains intact.

My point is that, over Europe to-day, it does not remain intact, and that it would be an act of folly to attempt its restoration now that Hitler has destroyed it. There is now, as there has never been before, an opportunity of constructing an international order; and the need of such an order, both for the secure establishment of peace and for the lifting of the nations out of poverty, is imperative. I have tried to state the case for attempting to create this new order; and now I am trying to make those who accept the need for it understand what it implies in the sphere of economic relations. You cannot have any real internationalism, or any real security against war, unless you are prepared to build up an international State and to put into its hands the essential instruments of economic control.

It should be easier for many continental Europeans to realise this than it yet is for most people in Great Britain. The independence of their States has been destroyed, whereas the British State remains intact. Moreover, Great Britain is, both politically and economically, only half in Europe. It has ties with the British Dominions and with the United States which draw it away from Europe; and its rulers hold sway over a vast dependent empire. Great Britain cannot simply confederate or unite with its European neighbours without regard for these other affiliations: nor is it easy to imagine all the countries of the British Empire—to say nothing of the United States—becoming members of a confederal society based mainly on the European continent. Even if we consider only the problem as it affects the British self-governing dominions—how does Canada fit into a pan-European order which excludes the Unites States, or the Union of South Africa into a democratic federation which refuses to assign men rights varying with the colour of their skins?

Difficulties of a formidable number and magnitude beset all projects of international union, whether they are confined to Europe or range over the world at large. While some 'federalists' are stressing the need for 'union now' between Great Britain and the United States, and others laying plans for a 'Federal Union' of Western Europe, another set of projectors is dreaming of a Union of Socialist Soviet Republics spreading from Vladivostok, if not from Tokyo, to the West of Ireland, if not to Vancouver and San Francisco. One learned projector even wrote to *The Times* to suggest that surely the obvious and right solution was for all countries to become members of the British Commonwealth.

The trouble about most of these plans is not only that they are mutually exclusive, but also that, the more they attempt to include, the less likely are they to achieve that unification of basic controls which is indispensable for real unity; whereas, the less they include, the more they leave open the risk of future clashes between the new great States or Federations. Moreover, it is unrealistic to consider the future political structure of Europe, or of the world, out of all relation to the military outcome of the war. Even if we assume a Nazi defeat —and except on that assumption it is not worth while for persons such as you and me to consider the future at all— the character of the new Europe is bound to be different according to the forces by which that defeat is compassed. As long as it was possible to assume the neutrality of the Soviet Union, it was also possible to assume a settlement, at any rate in Western Europe, in which the Soviet Union would play no determining part. It always seemed to me fantastic to suppose that the Nazis and the Soviet Union, on the basis of the totalitarian elements common to their very different social systems, would form any real or lasting alliance. It did, however, seem possible that the Soviet Union would be able to stand aside from the struggle, and that, at its end, the future system of government in Western and Central Europe would be settled without Soviet intervention. This was, indeed, always questionable, because it was quite on the cards that the Nazis and the West European 'democracies' would wage a war of mutual extermination to a point which would leave the neutral Soviet Union alone erect among the ruins of European civilisation, and therefore in a position to impose its own conditions on its exhausted neighbours. It was, however, also possible to assume a victory over Nazism which would not lead to this result, but would allow the democratic forces of the Western countries to define the conditions of the new order without Soviet intervention.

The situation became altogether different from the moment when the Nazis launched their onslaught on the Soviet Union. For from then on the part to be played by Russia in determining the coming European settlement was bound to depend mainly, not on the degree to which the Western combatants exhausted one another, but on the extent of Russian ability to resist and ultimately to fling back the Nazi invaders. If the Soviet power were to be broken by the Nazi onslaught, so badly as to be unable to reassert itself in the general settlement of European affairs, the creation of the new order in Europe would be in the hands of the Western peoples and their leaders, and the settlement would be shaped in accordance with the traditions of West European government. On the other hand, if the Soviet armies remain strong enough to resist the Nazi attack, and later to sweep back across Eastern and Central Europe when Nazism reaches breaking point, Soviet influence will plainly count for a great deal in shaping the new order, not only throughout Eastern Europe, but also in the West.

As it is beyond the wit of man to predict at present which of these things will happen, prophecies about the future constitution of Europe must be largely guesswork; and the various plans which are put forward are bound to contain a large element of hypothesis. In particular, the future of Germany itself remains altogether obscure; and this involves an obscurity about the future of most of the countries of Central, Eastern and South-Eastern Europe. If Germany were to have a Communist revolution based on the Russian example, it is scarcely open to doubt that all the lesser countries of Central, Eastern, and South-Eastern Europe would also have their Communist revolutions, and that there would arise either an extended Soviet Union covering all these areas in addition to Russia, or a second Soviet Union, modelled upon the U.S.S.R., but working under German leadership and with German industrial technique as the main driving force behind it. I doubt, however, whether, even so, the countries of the Western fringe of Europe would be merged in either of these political groupings. Holland might; but I doubt it. Scandinavia might; but I doubt it even more. France, I feel certain, would not; and Great Britain assuredly would not. We should get, in that event, an extension of the Soviet system over two-thirds of Europe at least, with the consequence that the remaining third, or less than a third, unable to stand alone, would have to lean upon the United States for support, and the leadership of the 'parliamentary', as distinct from the 'Soviet', *bloc* of countries would pass of necessity to the United States.

On the other hand, if Russian influence in the coming settlement is confined to Eastern Europe, and revolution in Germany adopts a 'Western', rather than a 'Soviet', model for the new German order, the situation will be altogether different. For in that case a democratised Germany, reconstructed under 'Western' influences, will become the natural partner of Scandinavia, Holland, Belgium, and France in building a new set of institutions for Western Europe on a supranational basis, and Great Britain, instead of being flung into the arms of the United States, will be much more powerfully impelled to join hands with a West European Federation, even if this involves a pooling of dependent empires under supranational control. Even under these conditions Great Britain would still feel powerfully the drag away from Europe towards the English-speaking Dominions and the United States; and, for this reason, the British influence in Europe might be used, not to create an effective European Confederation armed with real powers of co-ordination and control, but rather to prevent this, in order to make possible a dual position which would leave the British State half in Europe and half out of it, at the cost of preventing the development of any effective Union of the West European countries.

I am setting down these alternatives as cold-bloodedly as I can, for the deliberate purpose of warning my fellow-idealists against the temptation to put their faith in fancy pictures of the new European order. I am saying, in effect, that we simply cannot know what sort of order it will be possible to build up in Europe until we know how the war will end, and what will be the balance of forces in the subsequent process of resettlement. We can, at this stage, know only that some things cannot be made to work—that it will be futile and disastrous, even if the chance does present itself, to reproduce the old system of independent, national States, with a new League of Nations no more armed than its predecessor with real powers of supranational planning and control; that it will be indispensable to create, somehow, large units of planning and executive authority on a scale much bigger than that of the single nation; and that these large units will not be manageable unless their common government includes within its scope the key functions of economic as well as political co-ordination.

What it will be right to work for after the war must depend on what happens during the war; for it is of no use to work for the impossible, and what is possible will be largely settled by the course of military affairs. It is, however, fully legitimate to express preferences, and to act on them as long as they constitute a possible basis for successful construction.

Let me try to say, as frankly as I can, what my own preferences are, and what difficulties face me to-day when I try to shape them into positive policies. On the one hand, I can see no prospect of assured peace or prosperity for Europe except on a basis of Socialism—that is, of planned development, resting on common ownership and control of the key industries and services, and designed to use them as instruments of popular plenty and social justice. This makes me welcome everything that strengthens the power of the Soviet Union, as the one Socialist power in the world and the one example of highly successful supranational planning. On the other hand, I am not a Communist but a 'liberal' Socialist, with a passionate belief in the value of certain rights and freedoms which do exist substantially in Great Britain, in Scandinavia, and in certain other West European countries, but do not exist at present in the Soviet Union. I am revolted by cruelty and by ruthlessness in the pursuit even of plainly desirable ends: I hate totalitarianism in all its forms, and hate especially the totalitarian assumption that everybody ought to think alike. I value not merely toleration of difference, but difference itself, within wide limits, as an essential expression of the freedom of thought. I value parliamentary institutions to the extent to which they stand for freedom of public speech, freedom to criticise the Government, freedom to make the Government answer publicly for what it has been doing; and I want the traditions which have been built up behind these forms of freedom to continue into the new era. Therefore I do not want the new order in Great Britain or in Western Europe—that is, over the area which shares substantially in these traditions—to be built up on a basis which means ignoring them or setting them aside. I do not want this, even if there are other forms of freedom no less valuable, which our way of living has hitherto missed, but which can be fostered in a totalitarian type of democracy. I want to add the new freedoms which are being achieved for the masses in Russia, now that they have been set free from Czardom and class-oppression, to the older freedoms which we of the West already in part enjoy. I do not believe these diverse kinds of freedom to be incompatible: on the contrary, I regard the one kind as the proper complement of the other, and both kinds as realisable within a framework of 'liberal' Socialism.

The trouble is that these 'liberal' virtues and traditions are at present enshrined in the institutions of countries which are not Socialist, but are still dominated mainly by capitalist parties and have their economic affairs still in capitalist hands; whereas the will to social equality and to the pursuit of plenty through Socialist planning is embodied in the institutions of a country which has never had a chance of assimilating the 'liberal' virtues, and remains largely barbaric in its traditions despite the revolutions it has undergone.

Thus I am left wishing for the greatest possible increase in the power of the Soviet Union as a means of furthering the cause of European Socialism; but at the same time I continue to wish for a strong enough rallying of the forces of 'liberal' Socialism in the Western countries to impose its own pattern of cultural values upon the coming settlement. Some optimists suggest that war waged in alliance between Great Britain and the Soviet Union will, before it ends, so 'liberalise' Russia and so 'socialise' Great Britain as to remove the antinomy to which I have referred. I am very sceptical of war as a 'liberalising' influence; and I confess I see few signs of a rapid enough advance of Socialism in Great Britain to ensure that the British weight in the coming settlement will be thrown into the scales on the side of Socialism. My difficulty therefore remains, and I have no means of resolving it finally.

I have, however, like everyone else who is not content to be a mere plaything of fortune, to find a basis for action here and now; and, up to a point, I encounter no difficulty in deciding what this basis must be. It is so plainly to the advantage of the world that Hitler shall be defeated that there can be no two opinions about the need for giving the Soviet Union the fullest possible military and economic help. Moreover, beyond this, it is so plainly desirable, from my point of view, that there shall be a strong Socialist power able to influence the terms of settlement all over Europe that I cannot but welcome everything which strengthens the political as well as the military position of the Soviet Union. This, however, does not prevent me from wanting to make Western Socialism as powerful a force as possible, or from urging West European Socialists and progressives generally to lay their own plans for united action, and to base these plans on an attempt to ensure that the coming settlement in Europe (or at least in Western Europe) shall be 'liberal' as well as Socialist. If this means, when the time comes for acting, a clash of policies between the Russian Communists and the Socialists of the West, so much the worse; but I am inclined to think that the more successful 'liberal' Socialists are in establishing their own common international front, the easier it will be for them to come to terms with the Soviet Communists. For the Russians respect strength and determination; and the most formidable count in their indictment against the Western Socialists is that they have shown feebleness in working for Socialism and in resisting the onslaughts of the various Fascist parties on the liberal institutions of their own countries.

I can, therefore, as a 'liberal' Socialist, work with a good heart and conscience not only for the military success of the Soviet Union, but also for the increase of its political influence—provided that I am also working to re-energise the forces of 'liberal' Socialism in my own country and in the other parts of Europe in which the 'liberal' tradition exists. I believe, too, that the more I work with and for the Soviet Union the better is the hope of 'liberal' Socialism being revitalised. Whatever the ordinary British workman may think about the Communist Party—and, generally speaking, he thinks very little of it—he does think a great deal of the Soviet Union, and does regard it as a country in which 'Labour', instead of 'Capital', rules the roost. It was no accident that Lord Beaverbrook's announcement, placarded in the factories, that every tank produced over a certain period would be consigned to the Soviet Union led to a remarkable increase of output. The key workers do feel that the Soviet Union embodies, however imperfectly, an ideal which is fundamentally their own, and they will be repelled sharply by any policy which allows hostility to Communism to develop into lukewarmness towards Anglo-Russian co-operation. This was seen very plainly at the Trades Union Congress of 1941; and it appears more plainly still in gatherings of the actual workers in the munition factories.

This intense sympathy with Russia, as 'the workers' country', does not in the least imply a desire to reproduce Russian methods in Great Britain. These methods do not, at present, at all fit the British situation. They might fit it much better if, at the end of a long war, the British economic and political system had been brought to the brink of collapse, and the Labour statesmen had allowed themselves to become so identified with the toppling capitalist order as to be incapable of leading the country against it, or of building a new order in its place. In such a situation, British political opinion might take on the one hand a Communist and on the other a Fascist turn, and the Labour Party might be submerged together with orthodox Liberalism and orthodox Conservatism. But this would be likely to happen only under the named conditions; and it would imply a signal failure of the 'liberal' Socialists to rise to the opportunities presented to them.

I think no sensible person will want this to happen. In such a country as Great Britain—indeed, in any advanced Western country—it is very difficult to imagine Communism becoming really powerful without Fascism becoming powerful as well. The same influences would engender both. The dissolution of society and the collapse of economic life, if they would drive large masses of the working classes towards revolutionary Communism, would by the same token drive towards Fascism not only large numbers of the middle classes and of the capitalists, eager to protect their possessions, but also a big section of the lower classes—the natural 'thugs', the constitutionally servile, and the ignorantly venal. Fascism and Communism would grow side by side, and in the struggle between them, whatever its outcome, many treasures would be uprooted and much damage would be done to civilised ways of behaviour between man and man. It might become unavoidable that this should happen: a situation might arise in which there remained no way of settling the fate of Great Britain except by a struggle to the death between these two forces. But the amount of suffering which would be involved would be enormous, in a country dependent for the basic means of living on foreign supplies and therefore on an uninterrupted continuance of home production and of foreign trade. The balance of advantage in favour of a less bloody way of settling the issue is overwhelming, if such a way can be found. But it can be found only if 'liberal' Socialism constitutes itself the effective champion of the new order, and succeeds in enlisting the support, not only of the main body of the manual workers, but also of large sections of the technical and managerial groups and of 'progressive' opinion generally. This, however, the 'liberal' Socialists can do only if they succeed in giving their Socialism a constructive international, and not a merely national, shape and content; for the ordinary citizen of to-day has at length realised that he cannot have security except within an international order that guarantees its existence, or freedom except within an international order that effectively outlaws the disturbers of the public peace.

In all this, what stands good for the people of Great Britain stands for the other peoples of Western Europe as well. Under the prevailing conditions, practically our only means of contact with these peoples are by wireless propaganda and by occasional public pronouncements of such authority that it is impossible even for Nazism to suppress them. Our wireless propaganda should clearly be governed by the will to stir up in Europe, if not immediate democratic revolution, at all events states of mind which will prepare the way for democratic revolution when the chance comes. The same consideration should govern our public pronouncements—our declarations of 'war aims', and our answers to the notions put about by the Nazis concerning the new European order which they are seeking to cement with blood. We, on our side, must make *our* new order sound worth working for, and worth dying for, if we are to win the enslaved peoples to our side.

But how can we? For the Governments of our countries are not our Governments, and do not stand for the ideals for which we stand. Even where, as in Great Britain, Socialist leaders are in the Government, they are there under the banner of 'national unity'; and this means that they are not suffered to say what they believe, or to hold forth hopes to the peoples of Europe of the new order which they themselves desire. I am not quarrelling with this; for it is inherent in the very nature of coalition government. But if coalition necessarily muzzles the leaders who hold office in it, that is all the more reason why it should not be allowed to muzzle their followers, or the movements which have raised them to positions of authority. If Attlee or Bevin has to remain silent, that is the more reason why the Labour Party and the Trades Union Congress should speak out boldly, and why you and I should speak. For if we all stay silent in the name of unity, we betray the cause for which we profess to stand. We leave the enslaved peoples of Europe free to believe that we, the advocates of Socialism and democracy, have no message for them, and have nothing to say that cannot be said for us by Mr. Churchill, with the endorsement of the Conservative Party and with the Federation of British Industries and Mr. Montagu Norman applauding in the background. To be sure, we are behind Mr. Churchill in his will to root out Nazism, and we must do nothing but what will strengthen the war effort. But that is no reason why we should be muzzled: on the contrary, our greatest shortcoming in the war effort is our failure, so far, to speak plain words of comfort and promise to the peoples who are suffering under the Nazi yoke.

The Russians realise this, and speak out. Their propaganda has been magnificent, because they *can* speak out, whereas we let ourselves be muzzled. Why, no one is speaking effectively to-day to the British people—let alone to Hitler's prisoners all over Europe. It is time to make an end of this self-immolation, and to launch at once, on the home front and internationally, a Socialist crusade. It is time to appeal to the peoples, over the heads of their rulers, in all countries, and in spite of the opposition of those who cry out upon us that our first duty is to 'win the war'. Of course that is our first duty. But how do we propose to win it, except by getting the peoples—including the people of Germany—on our side? And how can we do this unless we are free to say what we mean, and to hold out to them real and constructive hopes? Now, with the Soviet Union in the field and the news of its magnificent resistance filling the air—now is our chance; and we shall be fools and blind if we allow it to go by on the false plea that the 'national unity' will be imperilled if we are allowed to speak the truth.

VI

TOWARDS DEMOCRACY

We often call our country a democracy, and contrast the democracy of our system with the anti-democratic totalitarian régime of the Nazis. But in what sense is Great Britain, or for that matter the United States either, a democracy? Hitler and Mussolini call them both 'plutodemocracies'—that is, countries dominated by rich men making use of democratic forms. Socialists and Radicals of many sorts have often said the same thing, though they may not like it when they hear it said by a person such as Hitler, who wants not more democracy but none at all. Hitler denounces democracy as a clear sign of decadence, and proclaims the *Führer* principle—the principle of leadership—in its stead. Socialists and Radicals, on the other hand, when they have denied that Great Britain is a democracy, have aimed at making it one. They believe in democracy, in a sense in which Great Britain is a very long way from having achieved it yet. They would nevertheless affirm that there are in Great Britain very important elements of democracy which do not exist in Nazi Germany or in Fascist Italy.

What are these elements? It is of no use to make the stock answer that Great Britain is a democracy because practically the whole grown-up population has the right to vote. So it has in Germany—and a precious lot of difference it makes! Hitler knows as well as anybody how to throw a cover of popular assent over his own leadership. The problem of getting himself voted into power presented no difficulties to him when he had already seized the power without getting voted into it. Nor did it take Hitler's dexterity to master that easy art. Plenty of petty Balkan politicians knew and practised it while Hitler was still struggling to overthrow the Weimar Republic. Once get power in your hands, and universal suffrage will not prevent you from keeping it if you are ruthless enough in its exercise. On the contrary, the popular verdict will almost certainly give you a nearly unanimous vote of confidence—if you make things unpleasant enough for those who try to vote on the other side.

But terrorism is not the whole explanation—not by a long way. A great many of those who voted for the *Führer* were enthusiastic for him and for his principle of leadership, which repudiated the right of the people to rule. Democrats believe that the people ought to rule—that is what the Greek word 'democracy' means. But what if the people does not want to rule? What if it cannot be bothered to rule? What if it, or a very large section if it, positively prefers being ruled?

Hitler asserts not only that the people needs to be ruled, but that it can be made to prefer being ruled, and that it does not, and never will, really want to rule. He asserts that our democracy is a sham, not only because rich men make use of it for their own ends, but also because it rests on false ideas about human nature. If the democrat retorts that the people *ought* to want to rule, even if in fact it does not, the Nazi answer is that it ought not, because it is fit only to be ruled. And the democrat who thinks that democracy consists in the right to vote has no answer, both because Hitler can concede that and then laugh at him, and also because he has no legitimate way of questioning a popular verdict which places a dictator in power.

Universal suffrage is not democracy, or any guarantee of democracy. It is, doubtless, one of democracy's natural instruments, but that is a very different thing. Democracy means that the people has power, and not merely the formal right to say who shall have it, as between the claimants who are able to force themselves to the front. That misunderstanding of democracy leads to the situation in which one ruthless claimant, having first bashed his rivals over the head, appears at the hustings of 'democracy' and demands an unopposed return. That is, in effect, what Hitler did in Germany, and Mussolini in Italy, and, I think, in effect, though in a different way, Stalin in the Soviet Union.

Do not imagine that these words are the beginning of a

diatribe against the Soviet Union, or against Stalin, or of a demonstration that, at bottom, Nazi and Communist totalitarianism are exactly the same. They are not in the least the same in any essential particular. But they both rest on the knowledge that voting does not make a democracy, and that he who places his reliance on universal suffrage as a guarantee of democracy is building upon quicksands.

The Soviet Union is fundamentally a democracy, and Nazi Germany is not a democracy, though in both countries the suffrage rests on a broad, popular basis, because in the Soviet Union the whole community owns the vital instruments of production and they are run for the people's advantage; whereas in Germany the means of production are owned by private persons who run them for their own benefit and for that of the political masters of the State. The Soviet Union is fundamentally a democracy, and Nazi Germany is not, because the Soviet Union is trying to be a classless society and to educate as many as possible of its citizens up to the highest point they are capable of reaching, irrespective of their parents' wealth or social status, or of any prescriptive right or claim; whereas in Nazi Germany the class-system persists, with only the modification that a man can rise into the rich and ruling class by assiduous service in the Nazi cause. There is in Russia, and is not in Germany, the idea of giving everyone as far as possible an equal chance; and with that idea goes the related idea that power and authority ought as far as possible to come up from below and not be imposed from above. Russia, as well as Germany, has in fact a 'leader'; but there is in Russia no *Führer* principle—no principle of leadership from above—but the very reverse, a principle that leadership should come out of the people and that this emergence of leadership from the people should pervade every local and functional activity in the Soviet community.

Let us come back to our opening question. In what sense is either Great Britain or the United States a democracy? We have seen that the answer cannot be that the right to vote is widely spread. That answer simply will not serve to distinguish these countries from those which are under Fascist rule. Try another answer. Great Britain and the United States have Parliaments, in which the representatives of the people meet to pass the laws. Why, so has Nazi Germany a Parliament—the Reichstag; and there too the 'representatives of the people' meet. Ah, but they do not pass the laws: Hitler does that. For that matter, neither does the British House of Commons, the popularly elected Chamber, by itself pass laws. The House of Lords and the King have to pass them too, and neither of these institutions rests on any direct choice by the people. Even if we waive that point, does not the Reichstag pass laws by giving Hitler power to pass them? That it should delegate all its law-making power to the Government, whereas the British Parliament, even in war-time, delegates only some, is surely a matter of degree and not of kind. Of course, it is *really* a matter of kind and not of degree; but you can say that only by escaping from the bonds of the dogma that democracy consists in a particular set of formal arrangements about voting and legislative rights. The truth is that democracy is that which works democratically—so as to give the people power—not that which accords the form and shadow of power without the substance.

If we desert forms and shadows for the real substance, what becomes of democracy? For, in that realm of reality, the people cannot have power unless it wants power and is prepared to go to the trouble of exercising it. Is Great Britain, then (for we will leave the United States out of the argument for the time being)—is Great Britain a country in which the people does want power and is ready to go to this trouble? No, and Yes! For it all depends on what one means by 'the people', and on the degree of wanting and of trouble that is to be regarded as being enough to qualify for the democratic stakes.

What is 'the people'? Abstract political theorists have often spoken as if it were a mere arithmetical sum of all the individuals who make up the community. This is unrealistic nonsense, which leads straight to the perdition of democracy. Even if each individual citizen goes singly to record his vote, and if 'the ballot is secret as the grave', that does not make 'the people' a merely atomistic mass of separate individuals, both because voting is not the foundation of popular power, but only part of the superstructure, and because men and women cast their individual votes under all manner of influences which proceed from their contacts with others—from the lives which they live in groups and associations, and not in Crusoe-like isolation. Even if St. Simeon Stylites had dropped his vote into the ballot-box from the top of his column, and no canvasser had so much as shouted up at him a single political argument, he could not have voted as an isolated individual unless his pillar had been shut off from sight of the world and his personal experience of social contacts before he rose to that sad eminence had been blotted out of his mind. We live unto one another, and not by ourselves alone. Our political action is influenced by a thousand contacts, past and present, more or less intense, organised and unorganised, realised and unsuspected in their impact upon our behaviour. We are 'social animals'; and what is meant by 'the people' is explicable only in a social context.

Long before universal suffrage rose above the horizon of political possibilities there were voices contending that the people should rule. Milton said so, amid the turmoils of the Civil War between Cavaliers and Roundheads: John Locke said so, or half said so, at the very moment of the English Revolution which finally dethroned the Stuarts and put the Protestant Parliament in power. Even Burke, who denounced the French Revolution and 'pitied the plumage' of the French aristocracy while he forgot the 'dying bird' of the peasant multitude, thought that 'the people' ought in the last resort to rule. These 'peoples', on whose behalf supreme power was claimed, cannot have been the same: yet there was—there must have been—something in common between these several ideas.

What Milton meant by 'the people' was, in effect, all good men; for he did not admit the right of the wicked to share in the control of the State. What Locke meant was the 'commonwealth' of England, expressing itself through the groups and associations which lay at the foundations of the national tradition—the assemblies of county gentlemen, the boroughs with their councillors and freemen, the traditional communities of village life. What Burke meant was not so very different, but had a different emphasis, laying stress on the function of the landed and leisured aristocracy as the element which bound 'the people' together and was most capable of expressing its collective will. Hardly at all before the great French Revolution did 'the people' come to mean primarily 'the lower orders'. Before that it meant everybody, or at all events everybody who was not specifically marked off from it—all the 'commons', if not king and lords as well. But after 1789 'the people' came increasingly to mean the unprivileged majority, and in the minds of some the poor as well as unprivileged, while others continued to mean by 'the people' the rich as well as the poor, provided only that the rich were not badged with rank as well as exalted by riches above their fellows.

The precise significance attached to the words 'the people' changed as the social structure altered. In the mouths of nineteenth-century Liberals they tended to become identified with the idea of universal voting rights as the basis of a representative system, and to take on an atomistic meaning. Catholic social writers, on the other hand, continued to use them to express the notion of a social solidarity transcending class distinctions, and including the conception of men ranged in their ranks and orders for the performance of varied social functions. Marxists discarded the phrase, because they repudiated the very notion of social solidarity, and set out to emphasise the fundamental importance of class in the social system. They spoke of 'the proletariat', not of 'the people'. The phrase degenerated in the parliamentary countries, coming more and more to mean simply the voters, to whom it attributed a mythical collective personality—mythical because 'the people' in fact felt not as 'the people', but in many different ways according to their particular groupings and associations.

'The people', merely as a mass of electors, clearly cannot rule. The electors can indeed decide by a majority vote which of two persons is to be elected to serve in Parliament, or for any other elective office. But the matter becomes a good deal more complicated when they have to choose from more than two, or when there are multiple constituencies. It becomes even more difficult when the real question is not that of electing Mr. Smith or Mr. Jones, but of returning a majority for this or that party. If there are only two parties, the electors can give one or the other a majority. Wherever there are more than two the electors cannot, simply by electing certain individuals as against others, necessarily determine what the composition or policy of the Government is to be. The French 'people' repeatedly voted 'leftish', only to find that 'rightish' coalitions still held office in their despite. The weakness of Proportional Representation is that it gives increased power to the electors to choose individuals they like at the cost of reducing their power to return Governments they like.

'The people' that can be of real importance in determining political affairs is not, even under universal suffrage, merely the body of electors. It expresses itself in countless other ways besides that of voting for Members of Parliament. Every strong and active body of feeling, demanding this thing or objecting to that thing, is an expression of the popular sentiment, and counts fully as much as any voting in settling how the State is to be governed. The opinions held in common by large bodies of Trade Unionists, Co-operators, Churchmen, Nonconformists, farmers, shopkeepers, teachers, professional men—these and many other collective notions and sentiments go to the making of the 'will' of 'the people'. So do the opinions of employers, financiers, landowners, and of any and all of the vested interests which exist within the social system. 'The people', in any widely differentiated society, thinks not one set of thoughts, but many conflicting thoughts; and it is impossible for any act of government to please everybody. Nor can there be a coherent majority which is pleased by all the acts of any Government; for the same bodies of men do not think alike upon all questions. Representative government based on universal suffrage is a particular device supposed to secure the maximum of assent for the actions of the Government; but to the extent to which it works in this way, it does so only because the Government allows itself to be continually influenced by the opinions, not of individual electors, but of powerful groups which are liable to make trouble if their wishes on particular matters are left out of account. Any Government has, of course, to displease some of these groups; but the Government which most fully expresses the 'will of the people' is that which keeps most closely in touch with what the groups are thinking, and displeases as little as possible those which on the whole prefer it to any alternative Government that is available.

The influence of these groups is proportionate *not* to their numbers, but rather to the strength and articulateness of their feelings and to their power to make trouble if they are thwarted. These factors depend on many things. In the 'plutodemocracies', a few bankers may be very important, because they are in a position to throw millions of people out of work if they 'lose confidence' in the Government of the day and feel like teaching it a lesson. A few newspaper proprietors may be very important, because they can make a large number of people feel strongly one way, provided that they do not already feel strongly in a contrary sense. Rich men usually count, man for man, for much more than poor men, because they have a much greater power of making themselves unpleasant, and are much more used to getting their own way. Organised minorities—even quite small minorities—can be considerably influential if they feel strongly enough to be willing to die for a thing, or be imprisoned for it, or to lose their property for it, or their means of living. The power of groups depends largely on their 'nuisance value', though there is also a power that is derived from the will to render useful service.

Now, these conflicting groups are by no means all democratic, or exponents of democracy. But they are 'the people', in the sense that they all contribute to the make-up of what 'the people' thinks and wants. 'The people' is not necessarily a democratic concept: its voice is the voice of whatever counts as an influence shaping, from outside the Government, the policies of a community. This voice may be either wise or foolish, either idealistic or merely self-regarding, either for democracy or against it. In effect, it is a blend of all these things; and its predominant tone depends on the distribution of real power. In a country of aristocratic traditions, the voice of the landowning aristocracy is the loudest, and often almost drowns the voices of the peasant masses. In industrially or commercially developed societies, financiers, merchants and employers make the greatest noise or utter the most influential whispers. The Churches put in their words, which are influential in proportion to their hold either on the governing classes or on the main body of the citizens, or on both. The 'voice of the people' is predominantly the voice of democracy where 'the people' is democratically minded and organised to express democratic desires. But 'the people', in itself, is neither democratic nor undemocratic. A party with a large popular following is not necessarily a democratic party: the 'voice of the people' is not necessarily the voice of democracy: even the voice of a majority is by no means necessarily a democratic voice.

It is indispensable to labour this point because most men at the present time, in the countries which have a tradition of representative government, tend instinctively to think of democracy as meaning the sovereignty of 'the people' and to identify democratic government with government which depends on a majority of votes. The truth is that democracy depends, not on any formal order of voting, but on the spirit that pervades a society. The most democratic society is that in which the largest proportion of the citizens want real political power to be widely distributed and are able to secure that it shall be widely distributed in practice as well as in theory. Democracy cannot exist except where the will to democracy is widely diffused, and the social structure such as to allow this will to be effectively exercised.

Democracy, it follows, is a matter of more or less. No community can be absolutely democratic, and none can be absolutely lacking in democratic elements. Some communities can possess a great deal of real democracy even under an essentially undemocratic constitution, where there are within it strongly organised groups animated by democratic feelings and prepared to kick hard against oppression. At the other extreme, a community can have a highly democratic paper constitution, and be hardly at all a democracy, because the citizens lack the will and the organisation needed to make democracy effective.

The existence of this will to democracy is not merely accidental and without cause. Historically, it has been based most often on a wide diffusion of property, or on sharp cleavages of nationality or religion between the rulers and the main body of subjects, or, in simple societies, on a natural equality resulting from the absence of sharp differences in wealth and capacity for power. But it cannot easily exist in a society in which there are many gradations of wealth and power, so that the extreme classes are very far apart but there is no sharp break at any one point between clearly defined classes—or at all events it cannot easily exist in such a society in the absence of alien rulers or deep religious differences between the rulers and the ruled. It is because modern capitalistic societies have mostly developed in this way that the will to democracy tends to be weak in them, even when their political institutions have a form appropriate to the exercise of democratic power. For in such societies, where the formal political institutions fail to reflect the real social structure, the will to democracy is apt to be paralysed by the alienation of the middle groups from the classes below them; and the upper strata of these classes, who are the best placed for advancement into a higher class, tend to side with their 'betters' rather than with the groups below them, because they cling to their petty privileges and their hopes of personal advancement more than they resent the domination of the smaller number who are better off than they are.

It is the mastery of this fact that, more than anything else, has reconciled the wealthier classes in capitalistic societies to the formal democracy of the ballot-box. The more clearly rich men recognise that democratic realities depend not on voting rights but on the spirit of the citizens, the readier are they to give the citizens votes instead of powers, and to side-track democratic feelings into mere electioneering. In Great Britain the Conservatives have extended the suffrage as often as the Liberals, and have not fared the worse for doing so. They knew well enough that, if class relations were sufficiently complex, they would not be faced by a combination of all the poorer against the richer classes merely because more poor men were given votes.

The elements of democracy that do exist in such countries as Great Britain are to be found much less in the constitutional laws of the realm than in the habits of the citizens. Democracy is alive to the extent to which the citizens possess the freedom of speech and association for common purposes, and are minded to use this freedom as an instrument for the expression of their own desires and to recognise a parallel freedom for others. These rights of free speech and free association have not been easily won. There lie behind their achievement centuries of struggle. Nor have they been at all completely achieved. But they do exist to a significant extent, and they do carry other freedoms in their train. Factory workers are much more free than they would be otherwise as workers because they have won the freedom to combine. Freedom of speech also carries with it a considerable freedom of personal behaviour. It breaks down limiting customs and traditions of uniform conduct and enlarges the scope for personal self-expression; which is again enlarged by the freedom of combination for those who share the same tastes. The battle for personal freedom is largely fought under cover of the battle for free speech and freedom of association.

Largely, but by no means wholly. For economic dependence in itself connotes a large measure of unfreedom, even where speech and association are free. The possession of enough property to give a sense of security in the everyday affairs of life conveys a feeling of freedom which no amount of liberty of speech or association can convey. The amount of real freedom in Great Britain is severely limited by most men's lack of security—by their sense of dependence on others more powerful than themselves for the means of maintaining their accustomed standards of life.

This limitation on freedom is not, however, the same thing as a limitation on democracy. It might, in certain circumstances, positively stimulate the democratic spirit by provoking the desire to put an end to it. To some extent it does this, or the Labour Party would not be a power in the land. But this process is very imperfectly effective, because the 'security' motive is crossed by so many others. Many men prefer an insecure superiority to a security which is based on all sharing alike; and many fear that in seeking a greater security for their class they may imperil such small personal security as they themselves enjoy. The spreading wide of petty privileges is among the best-known ways of combating the democratic spirit; and the society which has the greatest multiplicity of social gradations has also the most petty privileges to confer.

In such societies the spirit of democracy is very apt to grow dim. It has, however, to encounter another insidious enemy—hugeness. The sheer growth in the numbers of men and women who make up a society has a tendency to undermine democracy by increasing the scale on which everything has to be organised. Hugeness compels men to have too many neighbours. In really small communities democracy can strike easy roots in the knowledge, intimate and personal, which everyone has of everyone else, or at least can have for the asking, and in the small scope for grandeur which such societies afford. In the great States of the modern world, where towns have grown as populous as countries were once, and there is continual movement of population both within these great towns and from town to town over the whole area, association can very commonly not achieve its purpose unless it becomes nation-wide. National associations for this or that can indeed be broken up into branches which to some extent preserve the spirit of neighbourhood. But the coming and going involve much shifting from branch to branch, and check the development of an intense local life. Moreover, and more importantly, the large national association has to develop its own bureaucracy, parallel to the bureaucracy of the State. The national leaders and officers cannot be personally known to the majority of those whom they are supposed to represent. They become remote, superior beings of a different order—even in some cases of a different class; and the effect is to destroy the natural spontaneity of the voluntary group and to convert it into a mechanical instrument instead of a spiritual force. Thus, instead of keeping alive and fostering the democratic spirit, association itself becomes increasingly identified with the bureaucracy which leads it rather than with the main body of the members. In some concerns—for example, in great joint stock companies, and in large friendly societies and building societies—membership comes to be the merest formality, involving no sense at all of partnership in a common venture; and in other cases, such as Co-operative Societies and even Trade Unions, though there remains in the membership an active element alive to the affairs of the association and with a sense of community in it, this feeling barely touches the main body of those who belong to it, and they pay their dues and receive what is due to them with no more emotional relation to the association or to their fellow-members than if they were buying a pound of tea at the Home and Colonial or paying the weekly pence to the Prudential Insurance Company.

This makes very precious what does survive of real human grouping based on neighbourhood and personal acquaintance and personal co-operation in a common concern. It might be expected to make it much easier for churches to strengthen their hold upon men and women; for churches do to a very great extent preserve this basis of neighbourhood. Probably this fact does largely explain why organised religion did not, from the mid-nineteenth century onward, decline much more rapidly than it actually did. Especially in the poorest areas the churches and chapels did provide men and women with neighbourhood groups of which they stood greatly in need. Their decline was hastened in other areas by the diminution of the attachment of urban populations to any one locality small enough to serve as a focus for the sentiment of neighbourhood. When home and work-place lie many miles apart, and both are a long way from the urban centre where the main amusements and the big shops are congregated, even next-door neighbours cease to know one another. The home becomes a dormitory: the social life of the household is disintegrated: the outer world comes into it through newspaper and wireless and not through personal visiting of neighbours. The public house ceases to be a focus of local gossip and opinion, and nothing takes its place. The church's social membership comes to be only a fraction of its dwindling congregation.

How can men be expected to feel democratically in such an environment? They can still be roused on occasion to mass-sentiments which simulate democratic feeling. But the continuous natural democracy of persons knowing one another and co-operating regularly for common objects shrinks up and becomes the possession only of the few who are keenly conscious of the need for it, and go out to seek it, not so much for its own sake as because they have an exceptionally keen awareness of the need for social ideals. These few make movements, and are the movements which they make. The majority of men ignore them, except occasionally, when some great event so disturbs the normal routine of living as to send them groping for fellowship in an unfriendly world. The great slump in the United States sent millions there groping after associations that would give life meaning for them. War also shakes men's souls, and sends them in search of companionship and mutual succour.

In this huge, scurrying, uprooted world of ours, companionship is very hard to find, except on a purely personal plane. Some discover it in air-raid shelters, or in the wretched refuges to which they are driven from their destroyed homes in blitzed cities. Many more remain solitary, even in their troubles. The most remarkable thing about those who slept night after night in the London tubes was how little they got to know one another, and how little they talked or developed a common spirit. Man grows more solitary in his multitudinousness: 'the more we are together, the *lonelier* we shall be'.

And yet . . . how numerous are the men and women of the Soviet Union, and how buzzingly companionable! Something has been unloosed in the spirit of man in Leningrad and Moscow that has not been unloosed here. The Russian is by tradition a melancholy person: the Russian intellectual, as he is mirrored in the works of the great novelists, is certainly not gay, and the Russian peasant cheerful only in the brief space between drunkenness and stupor. But the Soviet worker is gay—or was till this latest calamity of war fell upon him, and I suspect is even now. Whatever may be said here of the 'undemocratic character' of the Communist dictatorship, the Soviet peoples appear to be very cheerful under it, and very companionable. They behave as if they liked one another, *felt* free, and were at home amid the hugeness of the new State they have built.

Can it, then, be that hugeness is not so fatal to democracy as I have suggested—that it is not fatal at all? Is what is wrong with us not the hugeness, but our failure to adapt our institutions and ways of living to it? I believe that to be the truth of the matter, and that countries supposedly democratic, which do not drastically adapt their institutions to the changed technical conditions, are destined, in their hour of trial, to find that their supposed democracy has gone bad. The Germans found that—but it may be alleged that democracy had no deep roots in German soil. I am not saying that it had not: I do not want to stop now to argue the point. But the French found it too; and the French were the great inspirers of democratic notions over most of the world. Their democracy went bad on them in the hour of trial. Would ours, such as it is, have gone bad on us if we had been as sorely tried?

We were tried, up to a point, after the fall of France; and

it did not. It rallied instead. For a few months in 1940 Great Britain was a more democratic country than it had ever been before—or than it has been since. There revealed itself, under trial, a certain toughness of the British people which enabled the new Government to rely upon it for the improvisation of immediate measures of defence. There was a great spurt in factory production; and for the time being nearly all sections of the community pulled together in a remarkable way. But this effort was essentially one of improvisation: of its very nature it could not last, because it imposed too heavy a strain to be borne for long. As the immediate peril grew less, there was a slipping back into the old grooves. The glamour of Mr. Churchill's war leadership to some extent remained; but the feeling of national comradeship grew fainter, and men began to think again in the old terms and to revert to the old antagonisms.

There is no cause for surprise in this; for in reality the measures taken for the defence of Britain did not overcome any of the old antinomies or make any fundamental change in the organisation of British society. The class-structure remained unaffected by them. There was no taking of industry—employers and workers alike—into the direct service of the commonwealth, no promise of a change in social relations either during or after the war. Parliament, the supposed embodiment of democratic representation, remained just as it had been—a ludicrous array of nobodies returned in 1935 in the train of Neville Chamberlain, without prestige or capacity to rally the nation behind them. The Opposition, too, was in a mess. Attlee, a good man in his place and possessed of social instincts, lacked altogether the qualities essential for leadership. For the rest, the Labour Party was manned largely by jaded old 'stalwarts'; for in the election of 1935 these fought the safe seats, while what there was of youth and initiative in the party mostly went down to defeat in constituencies that were unwinnable without an effective national leadership.

This inferiority of Parliament would have mattered less had not the war conditions brought about a paralysis of many of the agents through which popular opinion normally expresses itself. There was, to begin with, a quite needless and foolish interference with the normal working of local government. In many cases, local Councils handed over a quite unnecessary number of powers to their permanent officials or to emergency committees; and the normal meetings of Councils and committees ceased to be held. This meant that many local government activities vanished from public scrutiny. In addition, many of the most active councillors and many of their most vigorous critics were absorbed into emergency duties connected with Home Defence, evacuation, and other war-time services; and, with all elections suspended for the local Councils, the party machinery for the mobilisation of popular opinion was largely disbanded. The black-out—and air raids, when they came—interfered with public meetings; and many of the more active local politicians were drafted into the armed forces or kept working long hours of overtime in the factories making essential supplies. The regular leadership of local opinion was thus for the most part taken away; and in the absence of leaders there was no effective means of keeping the political consciousness of their followers alive, or at all events of bringing it to bear on current problems. The Communists, no doubt, kept going with their habitual energy; but their anti-war policy ruled them out of court until the Nazis attacked the Soviet Union and caused them to change their 'party line' yet again—and by then their tergiversations had so discredited them as to make the recovery of their influence a matter of difficulty which could not be overcome at once.

Not only in respect of local government did this paralysis of voluntary effort exist. It seemed as if all the energies of the country had to be put into winning the war, and there were none to spare for 'politics' in any ordinary sense. There was even a feeling that it was somehow unpatriotic to engage in any 'political' activities, and that criticism of the Government, even in matters of home policy, was to be avoided for fear of interfering with 'national unity'. With the leaders of all the political parties in the Government, and jointly responsible for its policy, there was no organised Opposition, either in Parliament or in the country; and attempts to organise criticism were resented both by the leaders who were in the Government and by those who controlled the several political machines.

Yet criticism was not necessarily factious, and, so far from proceeding from any desire to hamper the war effort, might well arise out of a will to get it organised more effectively. The standing debate between the advocates of capitalism and Socialism could not truly be put aside as irrelevant for the duration of the war. It was very arguable that, whatever might be the respective merits of the two systems in time of peace, Socialism was the right principle to work on for waging the war. A strong case could be made out for the view that under war conditions it was essential to bring the vital industries and services under a planned and co-ordinated control which could be achieved only by taking them over completely as public concerns. There was also a strong case for limiting all war-time incomes to what was really needed, and for rationing not only certain kinds of foodstuffs and other necessaries, but also the total income which any consumer was to be allowed to spend. If these things had been done, the war effort would have been greatly strengthened. But with all the parties represented in the Government, and nearly all the critics feeling diffidence about putting forward any view which the Government might reject, they did not get done; for the Government itself stood for 'national unity'. 'National unity' meant in practice not making any far-reaching change to which the Conservatives and their capitalist friends objected; and the Labour Members of the Government accepted this, and their fellow-leaders of opinion outside the Government accepted it too.

The consequence was that democracy went into cold storage, or at least one vital form of it did. For in deciding on public policy, it was a question not of what 'the people' wanted, but of what the rival political parties could be induced to accept. This meant in effect keeping capitalism intact; for if the Conservatives would not consent to the suspension of capitalist methods, the *status quo* held the field.

This situation is perilous both from the standpoint of winning the war and in relation to the future. I do not want to argue further now about the extent to which the retention of capitalist incentives, methods, and forms of control is hampering the war effort; for I have said what I have to say on that matter earlier in this book. What I have to urge now is that the suspension of the democratic practice of deciding upon policies by public argument is highly dangerous. In normal times there are advocates of various policies trying to get their proposals publicly canvassed and, if possible, taken up by the political parties. To-day the process of public argument is largely in abeyance. The rival propagandists have been taken away by other jobs; and the politicians are no longer arguing at the bar of public opinion. There are no by-elections except where 'freak' candidates make an appearance here and there; and there is at present no prospect of a general election until the war is over. Criticism exists—not a little of it—in respect of air-raid policy, food rationing, bad transport conditions, coal shortage, and a number of other problems which directly affect the general run of consumers. But this criticism is uncoordinated and undirected, and largely ineffective because it concentrates on surface results rather than on causes. There is political criticism as well, and a very large amount of vague political dissatisfaction and of hunting round for inspiration from anyone who appears to have some of that elusive commodity on tap. But this political criticism is also in the main abortive, because the established parties boycott it and the various Leagues and Councils and Committees which are hopefully founded in order to make it effective can find nothing for their members to do except talk, and no means of getting a hearing beyond certain narrow circles of mainly middle-class listeners.

Defeat in the present war would be not merely disaster, but eclipse to all our hopes. It would kill for ever the chance of developing the elements of democracy which exist in Great Britain into the dominant features of a new order based on the British tradition and retaining the real values which belong to that tradition. It would not necessarily kill democracy for good and all; but it would mean the necessity for a fresh start and fresh bitter warfare for its achievement. It would mean that the new democracy would be, not a continuation of past victories, but something essentially different—perhaps worse, perhaps better, but, whether worse or better, to be won only by fresh earth-shattering efforts and at the cost of generations of further suffering. It is worth a great deal to win the war, in order to begin the building of the new democratic order on the foundations we have laid already, rather than allow these foundations to be destroyed and new anti-democratic foundations to be laid instead, so that we shall have to dig them up again in order to lay new democratic foundations of our own.

The worthwhileness of the war itself depends on our determination to build well and truly upon the foundations which we are fighting to preserve. Were we to win the war, and then build nothing fit to stand, how much of struggle and sacrifice should we be throwing away! For if we beat the Nazis, and then rely on the old, battered house of capitalism to last our time and our children's, we shall be condemning ourselves and them, not only to present poverty, but to the disaster of living in an age out of which hope has departed, and in which everything gets shoddier and more makeshift from year to year as the rotten structure gives way at one point after another.

This building we are called upon to do is no mere matter of bricks and mortar, or of sound physical construction, or of the replanning of industry and finance in accordance with the requirements of an age of plenty. It is also, and above all else, a matter of the quality of the human spirit. If we want this new age to be unlike those which have gone before, not only in its greater power to produce abundance, but also, and above all else, in the quality of its citizens, we have to find means whereby the spirit of democracy, which is that of valuing every human being as an end and seeking to elicit what is good in him, can be given strength to stand up and assert itself in face of the hugeness of organisation. We have to enlist as many as possible of the citizens in the constructive service of the community—which is their best way of expressing what good is in themselves—and we have to apply this principle to every aspect of social life. We have seen in an earlier chapter how necessary it is to apply it to economic affairs, so as to give every worker the fullest possible chance of feeling and acting as a co-partner in the common business of production. This is perhaps the most important aspect of all; for a man spends so large a part of his waking life at work—and will do, even if the hours of labour are shortened as much as we can afford to shorten them—that the feeling-tone of his working life necessarily affects very greatly both his capacity for political citizenship and his use of leisure. It is impossible for a free political and a servile industrial system to go on side by side. Either the free political agents will insist on emancipating industry, or the servile industry will undermine the nominal political freedom, both by making men think and act as slaves and by causing them altogether to eschew the effort of social thinking, and put their leisure to merely receptive uses, devoid of creative quality.

But though the democratisation of industry holds a key position in the struggle for real democracy, it does not stand alone. It is also necessary to democratise every other aspect of men's living and acting together. In industry, as we have seen, the effectiveness of the democratic process depends on men being able, at the basis of the industrial order, to act together in small groups—small enough for everyone to know, or be able to know, everyone else personally—upon matters which practically affect their happiness and well-being. The same conditions hold elsewhere. If we want to diffuse widely among ordinary men and women a capacity for collective activity and an understanding of public affairs, we must set out to build our new society upon little democracies of neighbours as well as upon little democracies of workers. Just as the great factory need not be an obstacle to this—for it must be made up of smaller workshops and departments, each with problems of its own—so the great city need not be an obstacle. We shall never make the great city a democracy merely by electing a representative Council to preside over its affairs.

Such a body is hardly nearer to the ordinary citizen than Parliament is. The basis of local government should be the small, neighbourhood group of dwellers in, say, a block of flats or a single street or group of small streets. For every such unit there should be a common place of meeting—a civic centre in miniature, to serve the common ends of the group. That centre should be club as well as moot-hall: it should have its civic restaurant, and should contain someone to whom the members can turn for advice in any of the troublous concerns of life. It should be a centre for children as well as grown-ups, with facilities for looking after children when the parents are away, and with its playing field equipped for children's as well as grown-ups' games.

The entire population of this little commonwealth should be encouraged to look to this centre as the real focus of their collective life. It should be for them not only a unit of government—the basic unit from which larger units should be built up—but also a means for the expression of the civic spirit. It should be what the church has sometimes claimed to be to the village, but can never be, even apart from the decline of religious feeling, to the modern town.

I am convinced that unless we build democracy on such foundations as these, we shall not succeed in building it at all into the structure of our new society. Failure to do this may not kill the democratic spirit—for, as we have seen, that spirit can be very much alive under highly undemocratic constitutional conditions—but it will prevent democracy from finding expression in the political order or playing a constructive part in the work of the State or the city. Unable to play this part, the democratic spirit will fritter away its energies, and the State, deprived of democratic driving-force, will become an easy hunting-ground for self-seeking or windbag politicians, bureaucrats and jacks-in-office, and vested interests and predatory conspirators of every sort. The common people cannot govern in great things except by acquiring the habit of acting together democratically in matters more within the range of their direct experience. If they do acquire that habit, they can learn to manage great affairs also. They can learn to tell honest men from charlatans, wise men from fools, and men of courage from bladders of inflated cowardice. This choice of men is the key to the art of good government—not because all power ought to rest with the chosen best—far from it—but because good government consists in a partnership between honest, sagacious and brave magistrates and an active, intelligent and friendly body of citizens.

This, then, is the kind of democracy we must build. We must set about building it now, and not wait until the war is over before we begin upon our task. We must not wait, firstly, because waiting may lose us the war, and therewith our chance of building anything at all, and, secondly, because these qualities of active citizenship rust in disuse, and it is ridiculous to suppose that men who have let democracy slip out of their hands in war-time will be effective exponents of its spirit in the tasks of post-war reconstruction. We must, accordingly, seize every chance of forwarding the cause of democracy *now*.

We can do this, if we will. In the first place, we can refuse to allow politics to be put into cold storage, and insist, whatever the obstacles, on keeping up political organisation—on holding meetings, spreading about literature, and canvassing our neighbours' and work-partners' opinions upon the vital questions of the day. Secondly, we can, with full loyalty to the war effort, seek to focus public opinion on things that are being done amiss and that should be amended in order to bring victory nearer. We can refuse to be muzzled, or to accept the view that even if Mr. Churchill is the nation's best leader he must therefore be carefully kept from all knowledge of inconvenient facts. Thirdly, we can try, now that black-out and difficulties of travel keep people more closely to a single place, to organise small-scale activities that will meet their need for reassurance and inspiration in these times of trouble. We can be good neighbours, and can foster democracy by our success in making friends. We can break down the brick-box isolation which is the curse of modern living in suburbs and housing estates. We can do propaganda by living it as well as by talking it; and when we talk it we shall be listened to the better if we are living it too. *We must not consent to be shut up*—on any account. We must speak out the truth that is in us, because on making that truth prevail *now* the entire future of our civilisation depends. We must be democrats in little things, or our democracy in large things will be empty phrases.

VII

ACTION—NOW

SINCE the last echoes of Chartism died away in the eighteen fifties, we English have been on the whole a *quiet* people. We have had our political disputes, attended on occasion by no small amount of dust and fury—on the surface. But, save in the single instance of the Irish troubles, no political matter in the United Kingdom has for more than a century threatened to lead to fighting. Violent things have been *said* from time to time—by angry Republican Radicals in the days of Bradlaugh, by the Marxists of the Social Democratic Federation in its palmy days, and by Syndicalists and militant Suffragists during the years just before 1914. In the General Strike of 1926, to the astonishment of foreign observers, very few violent things were even *said*, at any rate on the working-class side. The General Strike failed, as it was bound to fail unless the Government gave way out of panic, or unless the strikers were prepared to make it, not merely a strike, but a revolution as well. They were not—neither the leaders, who incessantly proclaimed its entirely industrial and constitutional character, nor more than a tiny handful among the strikers themselves.

For a whole century Great Britain has been developing its institutions in a peaceable, constitutional way, with no more appeal to violence than a threat to create peers to overcome the obstinacy of the House of Lords, or an occasional fracas arising out of an industrial dispute. British Socialism, re-founded in the 'eighties after the eclipse of Chartism and Owenism, has grown up in this atmosphere of constitutional development. The Social Democratic Federation failed to attract the leaders of the working class, and the Independent Labour Party and, later, the Labour Party did attract them, largely because the S.D.F., whether or not it intended revolutionary action, did use revolutionary phrases and base its doctrines on a Marxian philosophy which was revolutionary in its essential ideas. The Trade Unions, on which the Labour Party is based, and to which its fore-runner, the I.L.P., principally appealed, developed under conditions which were strongly inimical to the growth of revolutionary sentiments. As Great Britain reaped the increasing benefit of serving as 'the workshop of the world', employers grew rich and workmen better off, from the same causes; and, though they might and did dispute over their relative shares in the loaf of economic progress, they had a common interest in doing nothing that could prevent the loaf from getting bigger at each new baking. Capital and Labour were co-partners—even if they were quarrelling co-partners—in a common enterprise of world exploitation; and, to the extent to which they acted on the principles which are supposed to animate 'the economic man', neither had an interest in pushing its quarrel with the other to the extreme limit. It suited the employers to make concessions when they were pushed, rather than stand out to the end against improvements they could easily afford; and it suited the workmen to accept these concessions, rather than die in the last ditch for more.

The religious conditions worked in with this accommodating temper in the economic world. The Established Church had indeed little hold over the workers; but the hold of Nonconformity was, until only the other day, very strong, and remains strong even now. Employers and workers not merely often attended the same places of worship—that was common in other countries. They attended the same *Dissenting* places of worship, so that the religion which they shared, so far from being tied up with the State and the aristocracy and the whole system of established privilege, was a religion of the opposition to these things. Wesleyanism, in contrast to the other forms of Nonconformity, made great efforts to remain within the Church and to disseminate 'Church and State' doctrine in political matters. But the established order would have none of its revivalist enthusiasm, and it was driven forth. Gradually Nonconformity became almost solidly the religious ally of the Liberal Party, as the Church was, less solidly, of the Tories.

As Liberalism ceased to be a party of permanent opposition, and climbed, under Gladstone, to political power held alternately with a reformed Conservatism, Nonconformity, its disabilities gradually removed, arrived at an acceptance of the basic conditions of the social system fully as complete as that of the Church, and was able to carry with it the main mass of its congregations, whose economic interest as well as their religious inclinations led them readily into the safe haven of Victorian complacency.

Of course, I do not mean that in this safe Victorian England everybody went to church or chapel, or that everybody was swayed by the same mixture of religious and economic motives. As we look back on that 'golden age' of British commercial prosperity, what strikes us most—as it struck Dickens and Ruskin at the time—is the festering mass of horrible poverty that was hidden by the imposing façade of Victorian comfort. These 'bottom dogs' did not, for the most part, go to church or chapel, or even, in the case of the Irish, to their priests, save on the rare occasions thought vital to salvation, if even then. They were left untouched till the Salvation Army went in search of their souls, and the Catholics, too, went slumming, amid the awakening of the social conscience that occurred during the 'eighties—I think, mainly as a sequel to the recurrent trade depressions which lifted the lid off the city stew. But, though religion did not, until then, trouble itself much about the 'down and outs', it did appeal effectively to most of those who were the natural leaders of the working class, and—here is the point—it was, by comparison with the religions of continental Europe, a democratic religion. The tone and temper of Nonconformity were drab; but this drabness had in it a strong element of protest against aristocratic pretensions. It did lay stress on the equality of men before God, not merely theoretically, but practically in the manner of its observances; and it was a potent outlet for the democratic sentiment, and a means of checking it from seeking a vent in violent outbreaks against the wealthy.

In this sense, religion was 'the opium of the people': it did offer otherworldly compensations which were alluring to men whose condition in this world was not so wretched as to drive them to despair, and was, on the whole, steadily improving.

The British Socialism of the 'nineties, the Socialism of Keir Hardie and of Robert Blatchford, was rooted in these conditions. Hardie and Blatchford—the latter much the more violently—broke away from organised religion. But their Socialism was in its basis ethical rather than economic in a Marxian sense, and was never revolutionary. They had realised, as General Booth and the other Booth, Charles, who instituted the great survey of *London Life and Labour* had realised, the mass of misery, beyond reach of ethical or religious appeal, which lay beneath the surface of Victorian well-being; and they had been deeply moved by it. Blatchford and Keir Hardie were led to Socialism much less by a conviction of the superior economic effectiveness of public enterprise than by a desire, too poignant to be denied, to remove this misery by striking at the causes of it, instead of merely seeking to relieve or to comfort. They created a Socialist movement of which the appeal was not mainly to the relatively well-to-do section of the working class to put an end to their own exploitation by capitalism, but rather to every decent person to join in an attempt to banish poverty and material wretchedness once and for all.

It was not in the nature of such a movement to assume a revolutionary form. It could indeed call to its aid fierce sentiments of indignation against 'sweating' employers, callous Boards of Guardians, and smug persons who attributed the sufferings of the poor to drink or perverse depravity. There was no lack of vigour in its denunciations of the cruelty and complacency of those who, having power in their hands, suffered such evils to exist without any attempt to end them. But the purpose behind these diatribes was to enlist all good men and true in a moral crusade for the uplifting of the very poor, rather than to incite the working class to a thorough prosecution of the class war. What Blatchford and Keir Hardie passionately wanted was to secure for the most oppressed victims of capitalism a more tolerable lot—that is, to lift them up to a standard nearer to that which the better-off sections of the working class had already achieved. They believed that this could not be done except by Socialism; and *therefore* they wanted Socialism. If thereafter they echoed Marx by urging that Socialism was an historic necessity, they did so by way of reinforcing their original argument, and not by way of replacing it with a revolutionary philosophy of class war.

Their main appeal had, however, of necessity to be made to the working class. The middle and upper classes they could approach only individually, in the hope of finding some just men among them. But an important section of the working class was already organised in Trade Unions, and the Trade Union movement stood in effect for many more workers than ever paid its weekly dues. Accordingly Keir Hardie especially set to work to win over the Trade Unions to his ethical Socialism, and to get them to join with his Independent Labour Party in creating a wider working-class party pledged to fight for minimum wages, maximum working hours, 'the right to work', and in general better treatment for the groups that were enduring the worst hardships under the existing order. Presently, the Trade Unions were persuaded, or half-persuaded, to the extent that a number of them joined hands with the I.L.P. and the middle-class Fabians to form the Labour Representation Committee. But it was slow going until a sheer accident altered the entire outlook. That accident was the Taff Vale Judgment, which, by threatening to take away the Trade Unions' right to strike, and therewith their power, brought them tumbling over one another into the L.R.C. as an instrument for securing redress. The L.R.C. became the Labour Party, and within a few years the Socialists' conquest of the Trade Unions seemed to be complete.

It was, in fact, very far from complete. The Trade Unions had come into the Labour Party not because the main body of Trade Unionists had been converted to Socialism, ethical or economic, but because they wanted certain kinds of social and industrial legislation in their own interests, and this was in the main included in what the Socialists demanded. The Socialists, however, also wanted a great deal more; and there developed inside the Labour Party a latent conflict between those who were driven on mainly by an ethical impulse to help the 'bottom dog', and those who wanted primarily to help themselves. There were, of course, good Socialists in the ranks of the Trade Unions. Indeed, most of the good Socialists came from that source. But the Trade Unions, as organised bodies, did not, in the period during which the Labour Party was taking shape, either become really Socialist in their collective policy, or, save in a very half-hearted way, put first the claims of the very poor. They were more interested in the Taff Vale Judgment than in the minimum wage, and in immediate reforms than in a fundamental change of the social system.

This dualism has never been fully overcome. The Trade Unions have become, under pressure of world events, a great deal more Socialist than they were in the Labour Party's early days. They now assent, without difficulty, to the proclamation that the Labour Party is a Socialist party, and to the drawing up on its behalf of an essentially Socialist programme. Nevertheless, when it comes to action, there is no strong Trade Union pressure towards Socialism. The miners, the railwaymen, and one or two other groups, for special reasons, do want their own industries to be nationalised. But there is from the majority of Unions no strong pressure towards public ownership and no clear differentiation between Socialism and social reform. Much greater practical importance is attached to any measures which will strengthen them in collective bargaining, and to getting concessions under capitalism than to replacing it.

Nor have the Trade Unions become thorough converts to Socialism in an ethical sense. They have, indeed, as a result of an experience of unemployment which has taught them that it may strike down the proudest craftsmen equally with the unskilled labourer, become much more ardent advocates of the claims of the unemployed—though even in this case with some suspicions of a policy which aids the non-unionist equally with the unionist. But they have still not much zeal for a minimum wage policy which would help mainly workers who are below the Trade Union level, and might, they think, hinder Trade Union recruitment; and some of them are also still inclined to oppose family allowances, not on the ground that they are not badly needed by the worse paid workers with big families, but because they might interfere with the established processes of collective bargaining. In practice, the Trade Unions are still concerned mainly to safeguard and improve the position of that section of the population that does join Trade Unions, rather than of the worst-off sections. And they still think more in terms of bettering the position of their members under capitalism than of fighting to make an end of capitalism and set up Socialism in its stead.

I am not saying these things in order to discredit Trade Unionism. Far from it. Trade Unionism has been my lifelong enthusiasm, and I hope I have proved myself its good friend. But it is futile to pretend that Trade Unionism is what it is not. It is, and it is bound to be, mainly an expression of the corporate grievances and aspirations of those sections of the people which it succeeds in enrolling in its ranks. It can be, and is, touched by idealism and by altruistic and ethical impulses. It cannot, in the nature of things, do other than pursue primarily the collective self-interest of its members, and this, as long as capitalism is a going concern, is apt to appear more consistent with making bargains with the existing system than with trying to change it.

It follows that a party based mainly on Trade Unionism must, not indeed confine itself to Trade Union objectives, but square its policies with Trade Union needs. It must give a place high up on its programme to anything on which the Trade Unions are insistent, and it cannot actively pursue any objective to which the Trade Unions are opposed. If its leaders are themselves men of strong, idealistic purpose, these limitations need not adversely affect the party in its day-to-day work; for the Trade Unions are open to idealistic appeals which do not conflict with their own objectives, as the great majority of such appeals do not. But if strong purpose and idealism are lacking in the leadership, the party is in danger; for it is then liable to be shut up within the limits of Trade Unionism, and it is impossible for it to sweep the country with what is no more than a minority appeal. Moreover, if a situation arises in which it is necessary to take bold decisions affecting the basic structure of society, the Trade Union tendency to think and act in terms of much narrower objectives may be a very serious handicap. It may set the party patching things up, instead of attempting radical reconstruction; and it may make the party disastrously slow in action in a crisis, just when speed is indispensable to success.

Seeing these difficulties, some Socialists conclude that the Trade Union basis of the Labour Party is wrong, and that it needs to find a much wider basis for its activities. But where is this wider basis to be found? One way is to seek it in an appeal to the wide body of discontent with capitalism that exists in all sections of the community, and is to-day wider than ever under the influence of war. The difficulty about this kind of appeal is that it has to be made for the most part to individuals, rather than to already organised groups, and that the common factor among these individuals, discontent with things as they are, has no constructive value until it can be harnessed to a movement armed with a clearly conceived programme and coherent enough to be capable of united action for the achievement of its ends. The countless societies and groups, with almost entirely laudable ideals and programmes, which come into existence with a glow of enthusiasm and then fade away within a few months, or at most a year or two, are a warning of the waste of idealism that can result from forms of political activity which fail to co-ordinate means with ends.

The truth is that, in large communities, it is impossible to base major political groups on idealism alone. There has to be, if they are to have either driving force or staying power, something else to hold them together. Political parties, however idealistic their ends may be, have to rest on powerful organised forces if they are themselves to achieve power. The great Liberal Party, in the days of its glory, rested on two such props—Nonconformity, and the merchant and shipowning interests which were devoted to Free Trade. The Tory Party rested, and rests to-day, on the highly tenacious aristocratic elements in British society, and on the vested economic interests which stand, not for Free Trade, but for State protection in its various forms. As the political interest of Nonconformity waned with the approach to religious equality, and also with the decline of the religious appeal, and as more groups of capitalists, in face of changing world conditions, deserted Free Trade for Protection, the power of Liberalism in politics evaporated, though Liberalism remained the personal creed of a very large number of persons.

If Socialists, in pursuit of Socialist purity, were to throw the Trade Union alliance overboard, they would be throwing with it their hopes of power. For there is no other strong enough organised group on which they could lean. Co-operation, as it exists to-day, is too narrow a movement to serve as a basis, though it can be a very useful auxiliary. It has, indeed, more members than the Trade Unions; but by the great majority the claims of membership are much more lightly regarded. Besides, those who criticise the Trade Union basis of the party have no desire to shift over to a Co-operative basis. They want to be quit of any basis, save that of personal conviction among their supporters. They are, in effect, asking for the moon.

The correct solution of the problem is not that of knocking away the Trade Union foundations of the Labour Party, but that of strengthening the idealistic elements within it, and at the same time promoting the reorganisation of Trade Unionism on more modern lines—on an industrial rather than a craft basis, and with the workshop rather than the branch as the fundamental unit. The Labour Party has suffered a grievous loss ever since it ceased in effect to rest on an alliance between the Trade Unions and organised bodies of Socialists, holding an idealistic gospel and seeking to permeate the Trade Unions with their gospel, and to change the structure and policy of Trade Unionism in conformity with their ideals. It owed what was best in it, in its early days, to this alliance—to the fact that the devoted service of the propagandists of the I.L.P. and the Fabian Society, which together formed its Socialist wing, was carried on inside and on behalf of a party expressive of Trade Union as well as Socialist desires.

This happy combination needs to be recreated. Some persons hope to recreate it by strengthening the individual membership of the Local Labour Parties, and turning them into the exponents of Socialist idealism within the wider movement. I too want to strengthen the Local Parties, but without hope that they can fulfil this function to more than a very limited extent. The Local Parties are, and must be, much more electoral agencies than repositories of an ardent Socialist faith. They have to take their cue from the electoral policy of the party as a whole, and to win as many votes as possible—which is by no means the same thing as making Socialists. They have, moreover, and are allowed to have, no central thinking machine of their own, distinct from that of the party as a whole. Any attempt to create such a machine for them is promptly stamped on by a National Executive which sees in it a sectional move, made in hostility to the Trade Union leadership and to their control over the party machine. Nor is this view wrong. The party cannot have its local electoral agencies kicking over the traces and claiming to act on their own.

This, however, does not mean that nothing can be done to improve the quality of the party without threatening its unity. It does mean that what can be done must be done without interfering with the party's electoral machine, or threatening the party with a rival within itself. The need is for a purely propagandist body, consisting of convinced Socialists and standing for Socialism and for spreading the knowledge of Socialism among the people, but neither producing its own parliamentary programmes nor taking any part, as a body, in electoral work. Its members, of course, will need to do electoral work, like everybody else who wants a party to win; but they must do it, not through the special body devoted to Socialist propaganda, but through the party's regular electoral machine.

Moreover, this body of convinced Socialists must set itself, as the creators of the Independent Labour Party set themselves more than half a century ago, to permeate Trade Unionism with Socialist ways of thought. Keir Hardie and his collaborators had in their day to wage a terrific struggle against the Old Unionism, whose leaders were not only Liberals in politics but also disbelieved entirely in the use of Trade Unionism as a fighting instrument of the entire working class. The Old Unionists regarded it as impossible to build up effective organisations among the less skilled workers, and thought of Trade Unionism as the bargaining machine of certain limited groups of skilled craftsmen earning relatively high wages, out of which they—and they alone—could afford to pay weekly dues high enough to maintain effective Unions. The New Unionists, inspired by Socialist ideas, fought hard against this exclusive conception, and were able to prove, by practical success, that such groups as gas-workers, dock labourers, municipal employees, and seamen could form powerful combinations, and that there was room inside the Trade Union movement for workers of every sort and kind. They were also able greatly to affect the policy and organisation of many of the older Unions, causing them either to open their ranks more widely or to form alliances with the new Unions for bargaining purposes, or even, as in the case of the miners, to create radically new forms of organisation. At the same time the old belief, widespread among craft unionists, that it was useless to demand legal minimum wages or legal regulation of the hours of labour, was gradually broken down; and the legal minimum, the eight-hours day and the state-guaranteed 'right to work' became the slogans of the growing Labour movement.

To-day, Trade Unionism stands in need of a fresh revolution in its attitude and policy. Just as the Old Unionism of the eighteen eighties had to give way because it no longer met the developing needs of the working class, so to-day the New Unionism which was created fifty years ago has become obsolete and stands in need of thorough reformation. There is, moreover, a remarkable resemblance in certain respects between the situation which Keir Hardie and John Burns and Tom Mann had to face and that which awaits the leaders of a New Unionism appropriate to our own time. The leaders of the Old Unionism in the 'eighties were incapable of responding to the new needs largely because they had come through a prolonged period of severe economic depression. During such periods it is impossible for Trade Unionism to advance to fresh victories: it can only hold on, to the best of its power, to what it has won in better times. Men who have led a movement through such a period of adversity, continually avoiding battle or facing defeat if they cannot avoid it, find it very difficult to adapt themselves to an essentially different situation. They have become so tied up with the policy of defensive collaboration with the existing order that they are usually as unable to change their strategy as France was in 1940 to abandon the obsolete military concept of the Maginot line. Consequently, they regard all who press for innovations in Trade Union structure and policy as dangerous and irresponsible troublers of the settled relations between Trade Unions and employers, and do their best to prevent the new ideas from taking root.

This is the situation in which Trade Unionism stands at present. The technical development of capitalist industry in recent decades calls for radically new methods of Trade Union organisation. But these new methods conflict with the accommodations with capitalism which enabled the Unions to tide over the difficult period of mass-unemployment and persistent depression between the two wars; and accordingly many of the leaders remain blind to their necessity. It is therefore essential to set out as clearly as possible the nature of the changes to which Trade Unionism has to adapt itself if it is to be a fully effective weapon under modern conditions of production.

(1) *The relative numbers of highly skilled craftsmen have declined, and the highly skilled craftsman has tended to become more a supervisor and co-ordinator of the labour of less skilled workers*

than an independent producer working on his own. This, of course, applies much more to some industries than to others; but it does apply over nearly the whole range of the light industries which have been expanding in recent years.

(2) *The old heavy industries, the mines, and the textile industries, which used to be the main strongholds of Trade Unionism, have declined in importance and employing capacity; and there has been a great expansion both of lighter consumers' industries and of clerical and distributive employment.*

(3) *These expanding trades and industries call for only small complements of highly skilled workers. In the main, their demand is for quickness, general intelligence, and a manual dexterity which can be fairly quickly acquired, and is fairly easily transferable from one industry or employment to another.*

(4) *As industrial processes have become more scientific, the demand for technicians has greatly increased, and a growing part of the skill needed in industry has come to be that, not of manually trained craftsmen, but of technicians trained in Technical Colleges or similar institutions*. These technical workers usually enter industry at a substantially higher age than the manual workers, and are often in possession of some sort of degree, diploma or certificate which causes them to regard themselves as belonging rather to the middle than to the working class.

(5) *Methods of production, which used to be differentiated mainly by craft or trade, come to be differentiated much more by type of establishment. There is apt, except for the minority of highly skilled workers, to be much more in common between workers employed in mass-production plants making quite different commodities than between workers making the same commodities in large and small factories*. For example, a worker who has been 'on the line' in Ford's or Austin's could transfer much more easily to a firm mass-producing, say, wireless sets or refrigerators than to Rolls-Royce.

(6) *Each factory, or at any rate each large factory using modern methods, tends to have a large number of problems common to all its employees, of whatever trade; and this factory community tends to supersede the older community of craft or occupation, except for*

the small minority of highly skilled workers, and to some extent even for them.

(7) *Management has become much more a profession, and has become much more divorced from ownership. The typical manager of to-day is not a capitalist, but an employee drawing a relatively large salary.* This change has affected the attitude of smaller employers who are also managers. Many of them now think of themselves as having a dual capacity, and recognise that works management is a technical job, demanding a skill which has to be learnt and is not identical with other 'business' qualities.

What changes in Trade Union structure and policy are called for by these vital alterations in the working of industry?

(1) The decline in the proportion of highly skilled craftsmen makes it much less possible to build really strong Unions on a craft basis, and leaves the craft Unions fighting a hopeless rearguard action for the continued monopoly of processes which no longer in fact require a high degree of skill. The consequence is that craft Unions lose their character as representing exclusively skilled and apprenticed workers without coming to represent effectively the main body of the less skilled. They thus tend to fall between two stools.

(2) The decline in coal-mining and in the heavy and textile industries puts what used to be the most advanced section of the Trade Union movement into a position of perpetual defence and frustration, which necessarily infects the entire movement.

(3) The fact that the expanding lighter trades can be learnt quickly, and that workers can shift easily from one to another, calls for a form of Trade Union organisation based neither on craft nor on industry, but wide enough to cover an extensive range of trades. This largely accounts for the rapid growth of such Unions as the Transport and General Workers' and the General and Municipal Workers' Union, which cater for this type of labour.

(4) The growth in the importance of the technical personnel of industry calls for the organisation of such workers in

associations acting in close association with the manual workers, or in special sections of the Unions catering for manual workers. The techniques needed in production are for the most part not special to particular industries; and accordingly the appropriate forms of organisation for technicians are for the most part such as to include technical employees in a number of different industries. This calls for special methods of linking up such organisations with those of the manual workers.

(5) The appropriate unit of organisation, and the place where the essential links must be made between technicians and manual workers, is the individual factory. It was natural for *craft* Unions to group themselves in branches drawing members of a particular craft from a number of different establishments, and for such Unions to concentrate mainly on establishing standard wage-rates and codes of working conditions for members of the craft over the widest possible area. Existing methods of collective bargaining are based mainly on these earlier methods of craft bargaining for persons possessing a common skill based on a common form of training, such as craft apprenticeship. The result is to relegate workshop problems and problems peculiar to a single factory to a minor place among Trade Union concerns. Modern technique, however, makes these problems increasingly important, and it becomes impossible for the Trade Unions to excite strong loyalties among the main body of workers unless they find methods of handling workshop and factory issues. Hence the development of Shop Stewards' Committees and Workshop Committees, which are, however, often frowned on by Trade Union leaders as soon as they claim any power or influence, because the leaders fear that they will use their power to undermine the old leadership, resting on national and regional negotiation about standard rates and conditions, and not on handling of workshop problems.

(6) In the industries which use modern mass-production technique, the workshop is the natural unit of organisation, with workshop groups linked up into factory groups, and

factory groups in turn into district groups. The skilled craftsmen and the technicians will no doubt need, in addition to their association with these works and workshop groupings, special associations of their own on a district and national basis, to represent their craft and professional interests. But the need for these associations must not be allowed to obscure the need for the more inclusive grouping of workers of all sorts on a basis of common employment.

(7) The evolution of management as a profession makes it possible for the manual and technical workers to become associated with the managers in the making and execution of plans for improved factory and workshop organisation, and for this form of association to be separated from the bargaining between 'Labour' and 'Capital' over such matters as wages, hours and general conditions of employment. Under these circumstances, the manager, *qua* manager, need no longer be regarded simply as the representative of 'Capital', and the way is open for collaboration between workers and managers as partners in the practical jobs of productive organisation.

To a limited extent, the things which I have suggested that the Trade Union movement ought to be doing under the new conditions are being done. The 'general' Unions, organising workers in many different establishments and industries, are to a large extent compelled to regard the factory as their unit for organising purposes, and not a few of their branches are based on particular establishments. But (*a*) they do not include the highly skilled workers, or the main body of those who are eligible for membership in more specialised Unions; (*b*) largely for this reason they often find it difficult to get a footing even in a big factory, because the more skilled workers have naturally the greater capacity for organisation, and tend to take the lead; (*c*) though they organise partly on a factory basis, they do not build the higher structure of their Unions upon this basis, or not to a sufficient extent, though in this respect the Transport and General Workers are a long way ahead of the General and Municipal Workers; (*d*) the suspicion of giving power to shop stewards and committees remains, even when use is made of them for organising purposes.

Secondly, despite this suspicion, the shop stewards' movement does exist in growing strength, and has been accorded some measure of Trade Union recognition. But (*a*) there is still a reluctance to admit the right of shop stewards from different factories to join together for the formulation of common policies, and a divorce between the shop stewards' movements and the local and national official machinery of the Trade Unions; (*b*) there is still too much tendency in some quarters to keep the shop stewards so closely attached to each individual craft Union as to prevent them from playing an effective part in a common organisation representing all grades in a particular factory; (*c*) the functions of the shop stewards are often much too narrowly circumscribed by Trade Union rules, and they are thus checked just when they are attempting to give practical effect to the desire for democractic workshop control.

Thirdly, the technicians have begun to organise in bodies of a Trade Union type. But (*a*) these bodies are still mostly small; (*b*) there are not nearly close enough links, either in the factories or nationally, between them and the Unions of manual workers; (*c*) many technicians remain hostile to Trade Unionism, both because they regard themselves as belonging to a superior social and economic class, and because they regard the Trade Unions as obstructors rather than helpers of technical progress.

Fourthly, the war has brought into existence, in most of the larger factories making munitions, Production Committees, which are obviously an important step forward. But (*a*) the Trade Unions have hedged round the elections to membership of Production Committees with so many restrictions as to weaken their representativeness, especially in view of the great amount of movement of labour from factory to factory made necessary by war conditions; (*b*) the line between the functions of Production Committees, concerned with the improvement of output, and Shop Stewards' Committees and Trade Unions, concerned mainly with the maintenance and improvement of the terms and conditions of employment, has never been properly thought out, so that there is great uncertainty about what Production Committees ought and ought not to deal with; (*c*) managements are still very often reluctant to have Production Committees, and bad at working with them when they are set up, largely because of this lack of clarity about their functions.

The outstanding problems which Trade Unionism has to settle in order to adapt itself to the requirements of to-day are, then, first, the establishment of the movement on a basis of *inclusive* workshop and factory organisation, and the creation of the right relations within this structure between craftsmen, technicians, and the main bodies of less skilled factory workers; and, secondly, the policy to be followed in pressing for the democratisation of workshop and factory control.

On the first of these issues, I believe that all highly skilled craftsmen ought to hold a dual membership—in a craft or kindred craft Union designed to safeguard their special interests, and in an inclusive general Union covering either a whole industry—where the lines of labour demarcation between industry and industry are sufficiently distinct—or a number of industries together. The miners, the railwaymen, the textile workers, the building and civil engineering workers, the printers, and some others can probably best be organised in separate *industrial* Unions, built up wherever possible on workshop or factory, pit or depot or job, as the basic unit of organisation. On the other hand, the host of workers in the metal, engineering and shipbuilding industries can move so easily from one branch to another that they seem to need a single Union, sorted out into sections each on a workshop basis, but covering all the metal industries together, and probably including also a large mass of other industries which use both the same types of less skilled labour and largely the same types of skilled workers and technicians for looking after their machines, conducting analysis and research, and planning methods of production and changes in output and technique. This points to the need for organising in a single general Union divided into industrial sections *all* workers except those in industries or services which have a clearly distinguishable labour force.

This, however, will clearly fail to satisfy the skilled craftsmen and the technicians, unless they have also professional associations of their own for looking after their special interests. Moreover, these craft and professional bodies will need to be organised on a basis wide enough to include men who have the same type of skill or technical knowledge both in the industries covered by the inclusive 'general' Union and in those which have industrial Unions of their own—for example, engineers in gasworks, mines, textile factories, or chemists attached to the lighter consumers' trades. These professional bodies would naturally deal with questions of apprenticeship and technical training, with craft and professional qualifications and standards of conduct, with professional salary-scales and special conditions of employment, and with any other specialised matters concerning the several crafts and professions. Such matters would be left alone by the general and industrial Unions, which would, however, stand ready to help in the enforcement of agreed craft and professional standards. In return the craftsmen and professionals would be members of the general and industrial Unions, and would collaborate with the less skilled workers in improving their standards and conditions and also in endeavouring to establish workshop democracy by means of Production Committees and in other ways.

The aim should be to make the Production Committees fully representative of all kinds of workers, technical and administrative as well as manual, and to get away from the notion of the Joint Production Committee in which the managerial workers, as representing the 'firm', consent to listen to what the manual workers have to say, and the technicians are as a rule entirely left out. Production Committees of this latter type can be only of very limited use: Production Committees of a really representative character, including technicians as a matter of course, can become most powerful instruments for the winning of democratic industrial control.

This is the kind of programme which I want the Socialist body that I am trying to describe to carry into the Trade Union movement, in the same way as Keir Hardie and his collaborators were able to carry their New Unionism into the movement half a century ago. The cry will of course go up, as it went up against the Independent Labour Party in the 'nineties, that the Socialists have no right to attempt to influence Trade Union policy, that their proposals are the irresponsible notions of armchair critics, and so on. But this must not deter the Socialists: nor will it defeat their efforts if their proposals are essentially right. Not even the most unbending Old Unionist of to-day can assert that all is well with a Trade Union movement which, while losing ground in the industries in which its main strength lies, has failed to win the allegiance of the great majority of workers in the newer, expanding industries, has failed to win over the technicians to its side, and is still trying to bargain mainly in terms of craft distinctions, many of which are becoming obsolete.

It is plain that the New Unionism which I have outlined, besides being the only appropriate bargaining instrument for the mass-production industries, is the kind of Trade Unionism that fits in best with Socialist aspirations towards democratic control. Socialists realise that real democracy in political affairs will remain impossible as long as, in his working hours, the ordinary person is treated merely as a hand, with no right to any share in the control over his working life. Moreover, Socialists want public ownership and control of the key industries, and a large measure of public control over such industries as remain in private ownership; but, emphatically, they do not want bureaucratic control over industries of either type. The best way of preventing bureaucracy is to have a lively and socially responsible democratic movement in the industries themselves, on a basis wide enough to include technicians, administrators and highly skilled craftsmen, as well as the general run of less skilled workers; and to entrust a large share in control to the representatives of this movement. These are the purposes for which Socialists have to work in and upon the Trade Unions, whatever Trade Union leaders may say.

I, as Chairman of the Fabians, who are now left in lonely isolation as the sole Socialist body of national standing affiliated to the Labour Party, hope that the Fabian Society may be able to play an important part in the performance of this task. Hitherto, it has been always a small body, composed mainly of 'intellectuals', and seeking to make its contribution rather by writing and research than by any widespread propaganda. As long as the I.L.P. remained within the Labour Party to do this wider work, it was right for the Fabians to specialise in their chosen tasks. But now that no one is doing this wider job, Fabian tract-making and research are left hanging in the air, and are unable to make their needed impact on the party as a whole. So I think the Fabians will have to go out and preach Socialism far and wide, if no one else will.

But why, I can hear many of my readers asking impatiently, why preach Socialism at all? Why tie up the gospel of love and fraternity, of decent dealing by one's fellow-men, and of idealistic will to make the world a happier place, with a very questionable economic panacea which is identified in many people's minds with most unethical doctrines of class-hatred and gross materialism? I hope my readers have not so completely forgotten what has been set down earlier in this book as to accuse me of either fomenting class-hatred or holding what they understand by a 'materialist' doctrine. The Socialism for which I stand and for which the vast majority of British Socialists stand is ethical in its very foundations: the very reason for it is our will to increase the sum of human happiness and to deal justly and kindlily by our fellow-men. That is why we are Socialists: that, and nothing else.

To be sure, our Socialism is not so much concentrated upon the misery of the 'bottom dogs' as was the Socialism of half a century ago. For two reasons: one, that something, though not nearly enough, has been done towards diminishing this misery; the other, much more significant, that misery now threatens all of us, rich and poor together, unless we make haste to set our social systems in better order. The pioneers of the 'nineties lived in a world which seemed to rest upon strong foundations: our world threatens to tumble at any moment in ruins about our ears. Our Socialism is therefore a hope of rescue for everybody, and not only for the poor.

However ethical our ends may be, we must have means of giving effect to them, or what are they worth? That is where the countless idealistic movements which blossom so hopefully and wither so fast miss the mark. Their leaders weave pretty patterns of reformation, but never ask themselves by what agencies their desires are to be made into realities. They wander about uselessly in a no-man's-land of political romance: they refuse to face the fact that the world is not ruled by personal ideals, save when they can become attached to dynamic movements. They form leagues of progressive persons, who meet together and pass elevating resolutions; and nothing happens. Nothing happens. Nothing can happen, because they have not so much put the cart before the horse as forgotten the horse altogether.

Let me say, once more, that it gives me no pleasure to debunk these worthy idealists. I wish their carts would go without horses; but I know they won't. I wish we could make a better society merely by dreaming of it, or passing resolutions about it. But I know we can't. I know that societies, like the children of men, are born out of pain and labour, and that we have to work for our ideals as best we may with the tools that lie ready to our hands.

These tools are men and women—and the groups and organised associations which men and women have made under the influence of their social environment. We have to take them as we find them, and to ally ourselves with those of them who are more favourable to our purposes than not. To the extent to which we have ideals, we have to seek out living movements in which some part of our ideals is embodied, however imperfectly, and to make common cause with these movements, or our ideals will remain without fruit. This is sometimes a hard discipline; for we cannot take men and movements as they are without taking the rough with the smooth, and accepting some things we do not want for the sake of others that we want very much. There is this element of give and take in all associative activity; and there is the more give in proportion as the social system we have to work in is itself diseased.

The times when it seems worth while to 'give' very little for the sake of 'taking' what we can are the times when only secondary matters are at immediate issue, and the wider questions of social right and wrong are barely under practical debate. On the other hand, in times of crisis it is worth while to 'give' a great deal; for the penalty of not 'giving' is enormous. For example, to-day, in a world faced with the threat of universal Fascist domination, it is worth while to make immense concessions in order to rally the forces against Fascism round a common objective and a common policy. It is criminal to stand on trifles, or even on matters which at other times would rank as of major importance, if as a result of our refusal the Fascists are able to conquer us one by one, without ever meeting with solidly united resistance. Similarly, in the work of building up the new order that is to prevail after the war, it is criminal to allow secondary differences to get in the way of effective unity among all those who want democracy rather than tyranny, and plenty rather than monopolistic scarcity, to be the basis of the coming society.

But this need for unity of the forces of progress is not a reason for vagueness. The drawing up of vague programmes which conceal unreconciled differences leads not to effective unity, but to quarrelling and desertion in the midst of the battle. Thus, it is of no use for Socialists, in an attempt to enlist Liberal support, to accept vague phrases about 'social control' as a substitute for their positive policy of socialisation. The basis of the new order must be either Socialist or not Socialist, or Socialist in some things and not Socialist in others. If it is to be partly Socialist, it is essential to specify in what parts of the new system Socialism is to prevail—not in detail, but in broad terms which will give those who accept the defined objectives a tolerably clear notion of what they are in for, and will serve as a sufficient basis for the making of explicit and practical plans of action. A woolly-minded progressivism, so far from meeting this need, is a sure means of leaving all the important practical issues evaded, and having no plans laid well and truly against the hour of trial.

The new order may be socialistic in some things, and not socialistic in others. But it must be either Socialist or not Socialist in its necessary foundations. It must rest, or not rest, on planning for plenty and social welfare, on collective ownership and control of the key services which determine the general character of the productive system, on collective control of the distribution of the national income, and on an attempt to achieve a social structure which will call for the active participation of as many as possible of the citizens in the work of political and economic government and administration. In these matters, at any rate, it is impossible to 'split the difference' between Socialism and capitalism without getting the worst of both worlds. For if we are to rely on 'private enterprise' to provide the main incentives, we must allow private enterprise a wide range of freedom to do the job in its own way. If we continually check and hamper it by attempting to control it without superseding it, the result will be that it will work badly—so badly that we may be driven to reinstate unrestricted private monopoly as the lesser evil. On the other hand, if we decide to invoke the incentives of social service under democratic leadership, we must ensure that the spirit of democratic service is not continually thwarted by capitalist influences. There is no reason why we should not socialise some services and leave others under private control; but the main driving force of the new society must be the one thing or the other, and not a compromise between them. Compromises may work in secondary matters: when it comes to the really decisive issues there is no evading a real choice.

It has been my contention in this book that Socialism, as

the main driving force behind the new social order, alone fits the conditions of the modern world. I have argued that the choice is no longer between 'free private enterprise' and Socialism, but between Socialism and private monopoly, and further that the dominance of private monopoly leads straight to Fascism and war, because monopolistic capitalism can no longer keep the peoples employed except by making or preparing war, and involves an international scramble for markets, materials and opportunities of exploitation that only war can resolve. I have argued that capitalism, which was once an expanding system, is now everywhere shrinking up and resorting to more and more restrictive and anti-social policies, and that there is no way of escape from this restrictiveness except by deliberate planning on a basis which will ensure a market for all that can be produced. I have appealed to technicians and managers, as well as to ordinary workers and consumers, to realise this in time and, instead of wasting energy on the defence of systems which are manifestly breaking down, to join hands in creating a new order, not on the prostrate ruins of the old, but before what is worth keeping in the old order has been irretrievably destroyed. I have called for a concerted attempt to build up democratic Socialism, lest, even if we escape Fascism, we have Socialism thrust upon us in undemocratic forms, and have to set about the remaking of democracy all over again.

I have, moreover, appealed to the readers of this book to set about these tasks not merely on a national scale, but internationally as well. I have tried to show that, as an ultimate unit of government, the merely national Sovereign State is obsolete in a world in which the key services need to be organised on a more than national basis, the exchanges of goods over wide areas call for more than national planning, and small States are doomed to military impotence and great States to vast expenditures upon armaments unless there is some more than national authority strong enough to prevent war. I have tried to show that these ends cannot be achieved merely by pacts among independent Powers, because they require positive collaboration and more than national administration and the development of a more than national democratic consciousness among the peoples.

The reiteration of these needs brings me back to the fundamental necessity—a wider diffusion among those who lead popular opinion of an understanding of the age's basic conditions and requirements. It is not enough for the national leaders to understand—nor will they, unless understanding is being continually pressed upon them by their own followers. For in a democracy leadership takes its quality from the quality of the led, or at least of that active minority which mediates between the national protagonists and the main body of their followers. These mediators are the key characters of any democratic régime; and the achievements that are possible to it depend on their intelligence, courage, and capacity for working together. It is the greatest weakness of modern democratic movements to have failed to give these pivotal men and women their due place. In the Labour and Socialist movement of a generation ago they were to be found in the Independent Labour Party and in the Fabian Society. They are still, some of them, in the Fabian Society; but it has only a small following. The work that the I.L.P. used to do for Socialism is simply not being done. Men and women all over the country are struggling heroically in Local Labour Parties, or joining forlorn hopes which offer them only a barren idealism empty of political reality. The workers in the Local Labour Parties are and feel isolated: there is no one to coordinate and guide their efforts on any save the purely electoral plane. The 'forlorn hopes' shed recruits almost as fast as they enlist them, because they can offer nothing practical or constructive to do.

Therefore, this book is a plea, not only for a clearer understanding of Socialism and of the ethical and democratic foundations on which it rests, but also, and above all else, for organisation of those who share this view of Socialism into a body of crusaders for the new order. It is, moreover, a plea for speedy action; for these are days in which the world's future is being settled for generations to come. We are at one of the great turning points of history: we must either advance swiftly towards Socialism or fall under the universal rule of Fascism as the final and most inhuman form of capitalist domination. The outcome of this world struggle transcends in importance anything that has been decided at any rate since the Bastille fell. But it also matters very greatly that, in ranging ourselves on the side of Socialism in this struggle, we shall carry over with us into the new Socialist order the real achievements of that liberalism which, together with Socialism, the Fascists are determined to uproot. The battle for Socialism is also the battle for democracy, and for civilisation itself; and the penalty of failure will be not merely defeat, but the total eclipse of all hope for ourselves and our children. Even so, perhaps humanity would rise again and reassert the great civilising values of toleration, freedom of speech and association, pity for the weak, and love of man for man. But how many generations of men would have to struggle before even as much of these things as we have known and enjoyed could be regained? For our own sakes and for our children's and our children's children's we cannot dare to let humanity slip down into the abyss by any slackness or vain bickering of ours. We have to find courage and a way of union that will give us strength; and I know of no banner behind which we can rally with the hope of victory save the banner of Democratic Socialism.

THE END

THE FABIAN SOCIETY

As I have called this book after the Fabian Society and urged those who agree with my general attitude to join it, it seems necessary to put in a few words about the Society itself. The Fabian Society was founded in 1884, and is the principal organisation of the British Socialist movement for purposes of research and educational propaganda. Historically, it is associated in most people's minds with the names of Sidney and Beatrice Webb and Bernard Shaw, who were primarily responsible for its earlier development. The Society itself is a national body, without branches; but closely associated with it are local Fabian Societies in many of the principal towns, and these act both as agents for spreading the results of the Society's research and as independent centres of local investigation and propaganda. It has also associated Societies in the Dominions, and many members both in the Colonies and abroad. Nationally, the Fabian Society is principally an organisation for the conduct of social research and enquiry; and it has special bureaux or sections dealing with International Affairs, Colonial Affairs, Economic Problems, Social Security, and other groups of questions. It has a Women's Group for the study of the social and economic problems specially affecting women; and it takes an active interest in Educational Reform. It publishes, in addition to its official organ, *Fabian News*, a research review, *Fabian Quarterly*, and two special journals, *Empire*, the organ of its Colonial Bureau, and *France and Britain*, devoted to the promotion of mutual understanding between the two countries. Its principal publications, however, are books, booklets and tracts embodying the results of its research and a series of propagandist pamphlets issued under the auspices of its Socialist Propaganda Committee. These books and pamphlets provide invaluable material for all who wish to study intelligently the contemporary problems of Socialism and social reorganisation. The Fabian Society runs a Bookshop for the supply not only of its own publications but also of books and pamphlets of all sorts, especially those which have a bearing on social, economic, and political problems. It conducts Summer Schools, Week-End Schools, and Conferences on current questions, and holds regular courses of public lectures. Anyone who wishes to know more about the society or to be put into touch with the nearest local Fabian Society should write to the General Secretary, John Parker, M.P., at 11, Dartmouth Street, Westminster, S.W.1.

EXTRACT FROM RULE II

"The Fabian Society consists of Socialists. It therefore aims at the establishment of a society in which equality of opportunity will be assured and economic power and privileges of individuals and classes abolished through the collective ownership and democratic control of the economic resources of the community. It seeks to serve these ends by the methods of political democracy."